WITHDRAWN

PRACTICAL GUIDE TO

OBTAINING PROBATE

Peter Wade

Emerald Publishing

www.emeraldpublishing.co.uk

Emerald Publishing

© Peter Wade – Revised Edition 2015

ISBN
978-1-84716-584-8

Printed by 4edge www.4edge.co.uk

Cover design by Bookworks Ltd

CONTENTS

INTRODUCTION

The saying goes that we can avoid everything except death and taxes. Maybe probate has the unique distinction of dealing with both these activities. We cannot avoid death but we can avoid taxes.

The proper regulation of one's estate can certainly minimise inheritance tax and maybe get rid of it entirely.

Life becomes more complicated by the day but it is possible without running up excessive legal fees to prepare a valid will and as an executor to undertake probate of someone's estate without legal help.

My definition of probate is very high-class administration. We are capable of doing it if we follow the checklists assiduously and keep a note of everything we do. If every piece of paper is accounted for and filed properly then probate should not be too difficult.

With the advent of computers, photocopiers, faxes and emails and the Internet these things are more easily undertaken by the organised amateur.

The minimum you will need is

1. Telephone
2. Computer
3. Somewhere to file all the letters.

I have attempted to take you through a typical probate transaction and to supply you with checklists, addresses, telephone numbers, and website addresses and draft letters.

I have tried to keep the text uncluttered by keeping the non-essential items to the appendixes. There will be notes in the text where these things can be found.

I purchased my first house by using a book although I did have the advantage of working in the legal department of a local authority. I knew nothing about practical conveyancing. It was a famous consumer association guide and I still have that copy on my shelves even though it was about 33 years ago. I am a great believer in *'how to books'*. They can at the very least take out this mystique of what the professionals try to wrap up as being very complicated indeed.

Wills and probate is not brain surgery but you have to follow a procedure precisely to get it right. You can save thousands in legal fees, which incidentally is doing me out of a job, but I will try and live with the rejection.

WRITING YOUR OWN WILL

Everyone over the age of 18 should make a will. Although in the public's view making a will is a straightforward matter it can have devastating effect if not written and executed properly and also if there is no will.

The safest advice is to always get a competent person to draw up and have a will executed for you. You can then rest assured that your wishes will be carried out in the event of your death.

Also if you execute it whilst you are fit and well there is less likelihood of it being overturned by beneficiaries claiming that you were not competent to do it.

If you are in any doubt about your own ability to draw up and execute a will you should get a solicitor to do it for you. At the very least your beneficiaries will be able to sue the solicitor in the event of him or her being incompetent or your beneficiaries missing out because of negligence. If you draw up a poor will they will only be able to regret for the rest of their lives that you had not taken competent legal advice which comes relatively cheaply for a straightforward will.

I often claim that I would happily pay the solicitor's fee for a will to be drawn up were I to be the beneficiary. So far I have not been called upon to pay up on that promise as no one has indicated that they want to make me a beneficiary.

As a practising probate lawyer I see a lot of heartache amongst families when they think the will has not been drawn up properly or they think they can overturn the will because the testator was not mentally capable.

Unfortunately the chance of inheriting does not bring out the best in people. Also families in those circumstances do not seem to enjoy themselves more than when they are falling out over money. We all believe that it would not happen in our family as we are not so petty and mercenary but in my experience no one is exempt.

We would much rather total strangers get part of the estate than let "undeserving" members of our own family.

Occasionally I get well meaning 'know alls' who say I am not paying your fees as everything will go to the wife when I die. That is partially true but intestacy trusts in favour of the children may arise which can tear apart a family. I suppose this boast is to prove how clever the speaker is.

I counter if I am in a difficult mood by saying: yes you deprive me of my fee but you are taking a risk that in the event of your joint death and intestacy your sister in law will inherit your estate. I have no idea whether the speaker has a sister in law but it usually encourages them to dip into their wallet to pay my fee for a properly drawn up Will.

We all have someone to whom we do not wish to leave our estate even if it's only the taxman. Or, on intestacy, ultimately the State. If you leave it to the cats' home provided it is a charity you save the tax and keep it out of the Chancellor's hands. A satisfying outcome

WHY MAKE A WILL?

If you do not have a will then your estate will be distributed in accordance with the rules of intestacy. Intestacy means when there is no will. A testator is the maker of a will.

Apart from limited circumstances you have freedom to leave your estate to whomever you like unlike some other legal systems such as in France.

You are entitled to go to the stationers and use a will form. The only problem with that is that it may work but any mistake in execution will invalidate your wishes.

Everyone should make a will and think about updating it regularly as your circumstances change.

****

1

Practical Will Drafting

Revocation of Wills

There are two main ways that you can revoke your will: by writing a new one; a formal declaration of all previous wills, by deliberately destroying the will.

Also the Testator must intentionally destroy the will or order someone else to destroy it in his presence.

There are statutory rules as to revocation of wills, and the most important ones being marriage and divorce.

Inheritance tax

Formerly Death Duties and Capital Transfer Tax, it is now one tax on death - Inheritance Tax.

The current level for Inheritance Tax is £325,000 (2015/16).

Any assets over that amount will be subject to a single rate of Tax of 40%. Therefore the first £325,000 is exempt, thereafter 40%.

The Nil Rate Band

If the deceased died on or after the 9th of October 2007 having a surviving spouse or civil partner-any part of the nil-rate band (under the death duty limit) that was not used on the death of that spouse or civil partner may be claimed by the deceased's estate.

This has the effect of doubling the nil rate band when there is a spouse or civil partner. At the current rate of £325,000 this means that the limit will be £650,000 before tax is payable.

The Chancellor has announced, in the July 2015 budget, that he is increasing the IHT allowance to £1m (for a couple) for the family home. People will not have to pay IHT on properties worth less than £1million. This will be phased in from April 2017. However, there are a few things to note. The 'Family Homes Allowance' will apply only to property left to direct descendants, children, grandchildren, great grandchildren and so on. Stepchildren will also count. The allowance will not apply to indirect descendants such as nieces and nephews. It is also suggested that advice should be sought when thinking of downsizing as the new IHT rules may affect your tax liabilities.

If you give away your estate and survive seven years, then no tax will be payable on the estate. There is a sliding scale over the seven-year period from:

0 - 3 years = 100%
3 - 4 years = 80%
4 - 5 years = 60%
5 - 6 years = 40%
6 - 7 years = 20%

Any year a gift made during a person's lifetime which exceeds the annual other special exemptions are known as potentially exempt transfers (PET's). These transfers are exempt from Inheritance Tax if the testator lives more than seven years after the gift, but if the testator dies within the seven-year period, they may be brought back into the estate. Therefore they are potentially exempt.

Equalisation of Estates

Transfers upon death between husband and wife are exempt and therefore in tax planning terms, if the whole estate has been left to the surviving spouse, then the £325,000 is 'wasted'. The idea is that each spouse uses their tax-free exemption by leaving at least the amount of the nil rate band directly to their children, or other close relatives.

This can only be achieved if the estate is large enough to allow the surviving spouse to have sufficient to maintain themselves.

Because the nil rate band has not been increased in line with inflation, more and more of the general population who would not normally regard themselves are wealthy are coming within the band, particularly on the second death. There are exemptions which can be applied on an annual and a lifetime basis.

Small Gifts

Any gift to any one person up to the value of £250.00 is exempt.

Expenditure out of Income.

Any gift out of Income which leaves you with enough money to maintain yourself would be exempt.

Gifts in consideration of marriage

There is a limit of £5000 if the donor is the parent of one of the marriage partners, and £2500 if the donor is the grandparent of either of the marriage partners. A gift made by anyone else is

£1000.00. There is an annual exemption of £3000 in each tax year.

These gifts must be made before the wedding ceremony.

Gifts to Charity
These are totally exempt, if left to a registered charity.

Gifts to Political Parties
There is no limit to the amount that can be donated to a political party.

Post Death Planning
DEED OF VARIATION
Within the two-year period after the death the will can effectively be rewritten to take advantage of the nil-rate Inheritance Tax band. This is made by Deed of Family arrangement. All the beneficiaries must agree to this.

BUSINESS PROPERTY RELIEF
In order to qualify for business property relief two conditions must be fulfilled

The testator must have owned the business property for at least two years before his death and the business property must fall within the prescribed categories

This will be ascertained by taking professional advice as to the definition of business property.

AGRICULTURAL PROPERTY RELIEF

The owner of agricultural property will receive a relief from inheritance tax if two conditions are fulfilled

The interest must be in agricultural property, which means farmland, or farm buildings used with that land.

It must have been occupied for agricultural purpose for at least two years before his death or owned the property at least seven years before his death during which period it was occupied by someone for agricultural purposes

SUGGESTED PRECEDENT WILL CLAUSES

COMMENCEMENT: Name and address of Testator

This is the last will and testament of me ^^^^^^^ of ^^^^^^^ in

the County of ^^^^^-

Formal revocation of all previous wills

I REVOKE all former Wills and Testamentary dispositions made

by mc-Funeral arrangements

I WISH that my body be buried/cremated-

Appointment of sole executor who is usually wife/ husband who is also sole beneficiary

I APPOINT my ^^^^ to be my sole Executor/Executrix and I GIVE AND BEQUEATH to ^^^^^ all my property both real and personal whatsoever and wheresoever absolutely PROVIDED that ^^^^^^ survives me by at least thirty days but if my said ^^^^ shall not so survive me I DIRECT that the remaining clauses hereof shall take effect-

Appointment of executor and alternative executor if first one predeceases

(1) I APPOINT my ^^^^ ("my ^^^^") to be the sole executor ^^^ of this Will but if that appointment fails (because ^^^^ dies before me or before proving the Will or is unable or unwilling to

act or for any other reason) I APPOINT ^^^^^ of ^^^^^^ and

^^^^^^ of ^^^^^ to be the executors and trustees of the Will-

IN THIS WILL and any Codicil to it the expression "my

Trustees" means its trustees for the time being or (where the

context requires) my personal representatives for the time being-

ANY POWERS given to the trustees of this Will (by the Will or

any Codicil to it or by the general law) may be exercised by my

Trustees before the administration of my estate is complete and

even before a grant or representation has been obtained-

Appointment of professional firm to be executors

NB charging clause

(1) I APPOINT the partners at the date of my death in the firm

of ^^^^^^^^^^^ of ^^^^^^^^^^^^^ or the firm which at that

date has succeeded to and carries on its practice and I EXPRESS

the wish that one and only one of those partners (or if the

appointment of ^^^^ fails for any reason to take effect then two and only two of them) shall prove the Will and act initially it its trusts-

(2) IN THIS WILL the expression "my Trustees" means my Executors and Trustees of this Will and of any trust arising under it-

(3) ANY POWERS given to the trustees of this Will (by the Will or any Codicil to it or by the general law) my be exercised by my Trustees before the administration of my estate is complete and even before a grant or representation has been obtained-

Appointment of solicitors

(1) I APPOINT as my Executors and Trustees ^^ and the partners at the date of my death in the firm of ^^^^^^^^^ of ^^^^^^^^^ or the firm which at that date has succeeded to and carries on its practice and I EXPRESS the wish that one and only

one of those partners (or if the appointment of ^^^^ fails for any reason to take effect then two and only two of them) shall prove the Will and act initially in its trusts-

(2) IN THIS WILL the expression "my Trustees" means my Executors and Trustees of this Will and of any trust arising under it-

(3) ANY POWERS given to the trustees of this Will by the Will or any Codicil to it or by the general law) may be exercised by my Trustees before the administration of my estate is complete and even before a grant or representation has been obtained-

NORMAL APPOINTMENT OF EXECUTORS

(1) I APPOINT ^^^^^^ and ^^^^^ to be the Executors and Trustees of this my Will (hereinafter called "my Trustees)-

(2) IN THIS WILL the expression "my Trustees" means my Executors and Trustees of this Will and of any trust arising under it-

(3) ANY POWERS given to the Trustees of this Will (by the Will or any Codicil to it or by the general law) may be exercised by my Trustees before the administration of my estate is complete and even before a grant has been obtained-

I APPOINT ^^^^^ and his wife ^^^^^ and the survivor of them of ^^^^^^ and any person or persons appointed by him/her/them to act after his/her/their death or incapacity to be the guardians during minority of any children of mine who are the minors at the date of death of the survivor of me and my ^^^^^^-

Specific Legacies including personal chattels I GIVE AND BEQUEATH all my personal chattels as defined by Section

55(1) (x) of the Administration of Estates Act 1925 unto ᴧᴧᴧᴧ

absolutely-

I GIVE AND BEQUEATH all my personal chattels as defined

by Section 55(1)(x) of the Administration of Estates Act 1925

unto my Trustees Upon Trust to dispose of the same as they in

their absolute discretion shall think fit or in accordance with any

note or memorandum which may be found amongst my papers

at my death-

I GIVE AND BEQUEATH to ᴧᴧᴧᴧᴧ such of my personal

chattels (as the same are defined by Section 55(1) (x) of the

Administration of Estates Act 1925) as ᴧᴧᴧᴧᴧ may within two

months of the date of my death select and I GIVE AND

BEQUEATH all personal chattels remaining after ᴧᴧᴧᴧ has

made ᴧᴧᴧᴧᴧ selection or the period for making such selection has

expired to ᴧᴧᴧᴧ-

Pecuniary legacies

I GIVE AND BEQUEATH the following specific legacies free of Inheritance Tax other fiscal impositions and of costs of transfer-

(1) ^^^^^^

(2) ^^^^^^

I GIVE AND BEQUEATH the following pecuniary legacies free of Inheritance Tax and other fiscal impositions:-

(1) To ^^^^^^^^ the sum of ^^^^^

(2) To ^^^^^^^^ the sum of ^^^^^

Pecuniary legacies to charities etc

I DECLARE that the receipt of the treasurer or other proper officer for the time being of ^^^^^ shall be a sufficient discharge to my Trustees for any legacy hereby given- *(Not necessary if using STEP provisions)*

(1) WITH REFERENCE to Section 31 of the trustee Act 1925 the words "may in all circumstances be reasonable" shall be omitted from paragraph 1 of subsection 1 and in substitution therefore the words "the Trustees may think fit" shall be inserted and the proviso at the end of subsection 1 shall be omitted-

(2) With reference to Section 32 of the Trustee Act 1925 provision A of subsection 1 shall be deemed to be omitted-

RECEIPT FROM CHARITY

THE RECEIPT of anyone purporting to be the treasurer or other proper officer of any charitable or other body to which any gift is made by (or under any provision of) this Will or any Codicil to it shall be a good discharge to my Trustees for the gift-

(Not necessary if STEP provisions being used)

UNDERAGE BENEFICIARY

IF any legatee hereunder (whether specific or pecuniary) shall be a minor at my death my Trustees may if they think fit pay transfer or deliver the legacy to such legatee personally or to his parent or guardian and the receipt of such legatee notwithstanding his minority or of such parent or guardian shall be a sufficient discharge to my Trustees for such legacy who shall not be further concerned as to the application thereof-

Residuary estate

I GIVE DEVISE AND BEQUEATH all my real and the residue of my personal property whatsoever and wheresoever not hereinbefore specifically disposed of unto my Trustees upon trust to sell call in and convert the same into money with power to postpone the sale calling in and conversion thereof for so long as they in their absolute discretion shall think fit without being liable for loss-

I GIVE DEVISE AND BEQUEATH all my property both real and personal whatsoever and wheresoever unto my Trustees upon trust to sell call in and convert the same into money with power to postpone the sale calling in and conversion thereof for so long as they in their absolute discretion shall think fit without being liable for loss-

Duties of executors

MY TRUSTEES shall stand possessed of the net proceeds of such sale calling in and conversion as aforesaid and my ready money upon trust to pay thereout my debts funeral and testamentary expenses and all duty and taxes payable by reason of my death and after such payment in trust for my said ^^^^^^^ absolutely and if ^^^^^^ shall predecease me then in trust for such of my children as shall survive me and attain the age of ^^^^ years and if more than one in equal shares absolutely-

PER STIRPES - Grandchildren taking the share their parent would have received if they had lived.

PROVIDED always that if any of my said children shall predecease me leaving issue living at my death who shall attain the age of ^^^ years such issue shall take by substitution per stirpes and if more then one in equal shares the share of my estate which his hers or their parent would have taken had he or she survived me-

RESIDUARY ESTATE

I GIVE all my property not otherwise disposed of by this my Will unto my Trustees upon trust to sell the same (with power to postpone sale) and out of the moneys to arise from such sale to pay my debts legacies my funeral and testamentary expenses and all duty and taxes payable by reason of my death and TO HOLD

the residue of the said proceeds of sale in trust for ^^^^^ for

^^^^^ own use and benefit absolutely-

I GIVE all the residue of my estate (out of which shall be paid

my funeral and testamentary expenses and my debts) and any

property over which I have at my death any general power of

appointment to my Trustees ON TRUST to sell call in and

convert into money but with full power to postpone doing so for

as long as they see fit without being liable for loss (and such estate

and property and the property which currently represents it is

referred to in this Will as "the Trust Fund")-

MY TRUSTEES shall hold the Trust Fund ON TRUST:-

(1)   To pay its income to my said wife/husband

for his/her life (but contingently on

surviving me for twenty eight days and

(2)   without becoming entitled to the income during that period except in that event) and subject to that :-

(3)   Absolutely for such of my children as are alive at the death of the survivor of my said wife/husband and me and reach the age of ^^^ years and if more than one in equal shares PROVIDED that if any child of mine dies (in my lifetime or after my death) before attaining a vested interest but leaves a child or children alive at the death of the survivor of my said wife/husband my child and me who reach the age of ^^^^ years then such child or children shall take absolutely and if more than one in equal shares so much of the Trust Fund as that child of mine would have taken on attaining a vested interest-

I GIVE DEVISE AND BEQUEATH all the residue of my property both real and personal whatsoever and wheresoever not otherwise disposed of by this my Will and any Codicil hereto unto my Trustees upon trust for sale (with power to postpone such sale) to pay my debts funeral and testamentary expenses pecuniary legacies and all duties and other taxes payable by reason my death and to hold the net proceeds of sale upon trust for such of my children who survive me and attain the age of ^^^^ years and if more than one in equal shares absolutely PROVIDED ALWAYS that if any such child of mine shall die in my lifetime leaving issue who survive me and attain the age of ^^^ years then such issue shall take by substitution and more than one in equal shares per stirpes the share of my residuary estate which such deceased child of mine would have taken had he or she survived me and attained a vested interest under this my Will-

IF the foregoing provisions shall fail then my Trustees shall hold my residuary estate for ^^^^ and ^^^^ or the survivor or survivors of them in equal shares absolutely-

FAILURE OF GIFT / SHARE AND THE BALANCE TO GO TO RESIDUARY ESTATE

IF the trusts hereinbefore declared of and concerning any share of my residuary estate shall fail or determine then from the date of such failure or determination such shares shall accrue and be added to the other shares of my residuary estate in equal proportions and be held upon the like trusts and subject to the like powers and provisions as those affecting such other shares-

SURVIVORSHIP CLAUSE

EVERY person who would otherwise benefit under this Will but who fails to survive me for thirty days shall be deemed to have predeceased me for the purpose of ascertaining the devolution of my estate and the income from my estate during the period of thirty days from my death shall be accumulated and added to capital accordingly-

IN this Will or any Codicil to it the Standard provisions of the Society of Trust and Estate Practitioners (First Edition) shall apply-

Extension of executor's powers

MY TRUSTEES may in extension of the power of appropriation conferred on personal representatives by Section 41 of the Administration of Estates Act 1925 at any time at their discretion appropriate any part of my estate in its then actual condition or state of investments in or towards satisfaction of any legacy or any share in my estate without the necessity of obtain the consent of any person- *(Not necessary if STEP provisions are used)*

IN ADDITION to all other powers conferred by law my Trustees may at any time and from time to time raise the whole or any part of the vested contingent expectant or presumptive share or shares of any beneficiary hereunder and pay the same to or apply the same for the advancement maintenance education or otherwise howsoever for the benefit of such beneficiary-

ANY MONEYS requiring investment hereunder may be laid out in or upon the acquisition or security of any property of whatsoever nature and wheresoever situate to the intent that my Trustees shall have the same full and unrestricted power of investing in all respects as if they were absolutely entitled thereto beneficially- *(Not necessary if STEP provisions are used)*

POWER TO INSURE

MY TRUSTEES may insure any trust property (including property to which someone is absolutely entitled) for any amount (including an amount which allows for increases in costs and expenses through inflation or otherwise) against any risks (including the risk of any kind of consequential loss and the risk of public or third part liability) and may pay the premiums out of the income or the capital of the property insured or any other property held on the same trust-*(Not necessary if STEP provisions are used)*

I DECLARE that all income received after my death shall be treated and applied as income from whatever source or class of investment or property the same shall arise and even if the property in respect of which the income arises is sold for the payment of my debts or for other purposes and whatever the period may be in respect of which the income shall have accrued and that no property not actually producing income shall be treated as producing income-

CHARGING CLAUSE FOR PROFESSIONAL EXECUTORS

ANY TRUSTEE being a person engaged in a profession or business may act and be paid for all work done and time expended by himself or his firm in like manner as if he not having been appointed a Trustee hereof had been employed by the Trustees to do such work including acts of business which a Trustee not being engaged in such profession or business could have done personally-*(Not necessary if STEP provisions are used)*

Attestation clause

IN WITNESS whereof I have hereunto set my hand this   day of   Two Thousand ^^^^

SIGNED by the said ^^^^^^ the Testator/Testatrix as and for his/her last Will and testament in the presence of us both being present at the same time who at his/her request in his/her presence and in the presence of each other have hereunto subscribed our name as witnesses-

SIGNED by the above named ^^^^^^ in our joint presence and

then by us in his-

SIGNED by the above named ^^^^ in our joint presence and

then by us in hers-

SIGNED by the said ^^^^^ the Testatrix and as for her last Will

and testament in the presence of us both present at the same time

who at her request in her presence and in the presence of each

other have hereunto subscribed our names as witnesses-

CODICILS

For Codicils........

IN all other respects I confirm my said Will

IN WITNESS whereof I have hereunto set my hand

this   day of   Two Thousand and ^^^^^^

SIGNED by the said   ^^^^^^^^^^^^^^^^^^^^^^^^^^^^^^^^^^^^
)

As a Codicil to her Will in the joint presence of us both)

Present at the same time who at her request in her)

presence and in the presence of each other have)

hereunto subscribed our names as witnesses-)

TRUSTS

This is an area of law which can confuse the person in the street as it is a term that is used but not fully understood. It is in effect a legal device by which assets may be held on behalf of another.

The most basic trust is when a person under 18 who cannot give a valid receipt has assets held on his or her behalf until they reach the age of majority. Before the age of 18 the assets will be held by trustees and during that time the assets will be held on trust.

TRUSTEES

These are the people who have control of the property and take responsibility for the running of the trust.

BENEFICIARIES

These are the people who have the benefit of the trusts

WHY A TRUST SHOULD BE CREATED

➢ They are used for a variety of purposes

➢ To preserve assets which people retain in the family from being dissipated.

- ➢ As previously mentioned for land and other property to be held on behalf of a child who is incapable of holding such property in their own right. This arises because a minor cannot give a valid receipt for property.
- ➢ To create a pension fund
- ➢ To operate investments on behalf of others such as unit trusts
- ➢ As a tax saving device.

The situations where a trust might arise are as follows

Children

If you wish to make a gift to a child then a trust is necessary for legal reasons.

LIFE INTERESTS

If the testator wishes to leave property to another to be held by them during their lifetime and thereafter to another.

This would arise if say on a second marriage the testator wanted to allow his wife to reside in the matrimonial home and once she died the property to go to his children. The wife would be what is known as the life tenant and has the right to occupy the property during her life time. The wife therefore merely has the life interest and the property is held on trust for both her and the children

CONTINGENT INTERESTS

This is when a gift is given on a condition or contingent basis. The most common example is when a gift is made to someone until they achieve a certain age such as 21 or 25.

If a gift is given immediately is known as vested. When there is a condition it is contingent that is awaiting the passing of some event on this occasion the age of 21 or 25.

DIFFERENT TYPES OF TRUSTS

THE DISCRETIONARY TRUST

This can be used for tax planning purposes. It gives the trustees the right that is the discretion to deal with the property in the trust as they see fit.

THE ACCUMULATION AND MAINTENANCE TRUST

These are used for the benefit of children and grandchildren

THE INTEREST IN POSSESSION TRUST

This is where the beneficiaries have the right to use the property.

WHAT CAN THE TRUSTEES DO?

The trustees' powers come from a variety of sources being from the trust deed itself. Statutory authority and common law authority.

Appropriation

➢ Apportionment

➢ Investment

➤ Maintenance of a child

➤ Advancement of capital

➤ The relationship between trustees and beneficiaries

➤ Trusts and saving inheritance tax

****

2

Enduring Powers of Attorney and Living Wills

Previously powers of attorney lapsed when the donor (that is the person giving the power) became mentally incapable. This would then involve anyone who wanted to deal the donor affairs in an application to the Court of Protection. This could be expensive and time consuming.

The other powers of attorney still exist under the Trustee Act 1925 or Powers of Attorney Act 1971. This could have the affect of terminating the appointment at the time when it might be most needed that is when the donor becomes mentally incapable.

The Enduring Powers of Attorney Act 1985 created the concept of Enduring Power of Attorney. This means once the power has been granted that it will not be terminated on the mental incapacity of the donor.

An enduring power of attorney can be created in the following circumstances.

> ➤ The donor must be 18 that is an adult with mental capacity. They must understand the nature and extent of the power. They must understand that he attorney will be able to control the donor's affairs and continue if the donor becomes mentally incapable.

More than one attorney can be appointed. Joint attorneys can act as either jointly or severally or just jointly.

Joint means that they must act together and if one dies becomes bankrupt or loses capacity then the power ceases to exist.

Jointly and severally means that they can act independently of each. The power still exists even if the other attorney becomes incapable through bankruptcy death or incapacity

In the event of loss of mental incapacity the attorney must then register it with the Court of Protection

An enduring power of attorney may just give a specific authority to act in a certain matter. In the event of a general authority than the attorney may act in any matter that is lawful for the donor to do, otherwise the power is limited to a specific activity.

An Enduring Power of Attorney only covers legal and financial matters, it does not confer authority in respect of medical decisions. A valid EPA can only be created if the document complies with the various requirements, such as being in the form prescribed by the 1990 regulations. The form incorporates the prescribed explanatory information together with all the relevant marginal notes. It must be executed in the prescribed manner by both the donor and or the attorney. In each case in the presence of an independent witness.

Registration of the EPA with the Court of Protection

In the event of the donor becoming incapacitated mentally, the attorney is unable to act until it has been registered with the Court of Protection. This imposes special duties on the attorney which arise once the attorney has reason to believe the donor is or is becoming mentally incapable.

The attorney is required to notify the donor and certain specified relatives of his intention to apply to the Court of Protection for registration. This includes husband or wife, children, parents, brothers, sisters, widow or widower and donor's grandchildren. There is a minimum number of three who must be informed.

Effective registration re-validates the Power of Attorney and restores to the attorney the powers granted by the EPA.

Once registered the donor can no longer revoke extend or restrict the extent of the EPA.

An EPA should be given in circumstances such as when they are intending to be absent abroad, and or at the same time as making a will.

Living Wills

These are also known as advanced directives, and are intended to allow individuals to specify the nature of any medical treatment that would or not be acceptable to them in the event of their losing capacity. Although called a living will, it is not actually any form of will in the legal sense.

****

3

Before The Grant of Probate

Administration of the estate

This is a general term relating to the winding up of the estate. It has to be done whether there is a will and executors are appointed or if there is no will and an administrator takes over the duties of the winding up the estate. The estate is of course all the assets and liabilities of the deceased. The public tends to think of an estate as meaning only freehold land as in a landed estate. Lawyers of course mean all the deceased's worldly goods. Whether freehold leasehold or personal

Immediate steps

Registration of the death

Normally the lawyers will not be involved in the registration of the death but if you do any amount of probate you will be called upon to do it because there are no close relatives or the firm are the executors.

The responsibility of registering the death is usually upon a relative but any person present may undertake it. When the solicitor is the executor then he/ she can discharge the duty.

It must be registered in the district where the death took place or the body was found.

The death should be registered within five days but an extension can be granted.

The procedure is that the registrar will require a medical certificate of the cause of death on occasions this is sent directly to the registrar and all you need do is make an appointment.

The registrar will require details of the date and place of birth and whether or not the deceased was or had been married...

As a precaution if you hold the will make sure the names that you register are the same as the names on the will as you may have problems later on when making an application for probate.

You will have to personally check the details and sign together with paying the fee. Obtain further copies of the death certificate as necessary.

The death certificate is a certified copy of the entry of death on the register. Each copy will be £7.00 (can change between local authority areas).

Disposal of the body

It cannot be disposed off until the death has been registered and a green disposal certificate authorising whether it is a burial or cremation.

If the coroner is involved there may be delay in the registration of the death.

Any wishes by the deceased as to the disposal of the body is merely a wish and is not legally binding but most executors will respect the deceased's wishes

Funeral

It is not technically part of the executor's duties to arrange a funeral but the executor has the duty to dispose of the body. As he will be responsible for the costs out of the estate it is usual for the executor to at least be consulted.

The direct costs of the funeral such as church, cemetery and cremation fees will be testamentary and administration expenses but not refreshments for mourners. Any payment for those out of the estate will need the permission of the residuary beneficiaries.

Burial

The funeral director makes arrangement for the burial of the body. Bodies may be buried elsewhere with permission of the local authority.

Headstones may only be erected with the permission of the priest in charge there is no automatic right to a headstone. Again the cost of the headstone will not normally be regarded as a testamentary expense. Care should be taken before disposing of all the assets of the estate that sufficient money has been held back to pay for this at a later date. An estimate will be given but a margin should be retained as it is very embarrassing at a later date to have to ask the beneficiaries to pay when they think the estate has been wound up.

Dealing with assets where no grant is required

These include

1.   Nominated property

2.   Property held on a joint tenancy: this would include land, bank accounts and building society accounts. Joint shareholdings.

3.   Life policies written in trust. Although it can be transferred immediately it does not mean that it will not be subject to Inheritance tax if it comes within the tax limit.

Obtaining the will

Solicitors and banks will only normally produce the Will on production of the death certificate and authority from the executors.

Care should be taken that it is the last Will.

With the executors instructions you should send copies of the Will to the residuary beneficiaries.

Taking possession of the deceased persons estate

You should take possession of anything of a financial nature relating the deceased's estate which ranges from actual cash to title deeds.

It is good practice when receiving items from the relatives to produce a comprehensive checklist. Send a copy of the schedule to the relatives as soon as possible. This will form the basis of the estate account. Also it will resolve any future problems as you can quite rightly claim that you only have possession of the items that are on the checklist. Try not to take possession of items that will give you problems in storing as the beneficiaries will look to you to keep them safe. Give back all bags, cases etc as otherwise your office/home will end up looking like a left luggage office and you will never know if ever when or how to dispose of these items. They may turn out to be family heirlooms. If any items are collected during the administration, be absolutely scrupulous about asking for receipts before they leave your possession. If in doubt about anyone's authority or identity make sure you check it before parting with the items.

These are all precautions to keep down any potential complaints.

There is circumstance when assets may turn up later and an amended account can be submitted to HMRC. You should impress on the executors / administrators their duty to give a full and frank disclosure of the estate to HM Revenue and Customs, similarly with their duty to the beneficiaries.

The more detailed and evidential your account the less likely you are to have an enquiry from the revenue if all values are backed up by professional and current valuations your clients will have discharged their duties to the best of their abilities.

Practical considerations

1.   secure any freehold or leasehold property. Obtain keys arrange for them to be locked etc.

2.   disconnection or inform utilities such as water gas electricity.

3.   all deliveries have been stopped or post-redirected.

Insurance

Check there is an insurance policy in existence and contact insurance company about the interim arrangements.

Powers of Personal representatives before the grant

<u>Executors</u>

An executor's powers come from the death and the Will. The grant of probate is merely a confirmation to those powers. In reality the power is restricted by the fact that any other parties holding the assets will not release the money until a grant of probate has been produced.

<u>Administrators</u>

Their powers derive from the grant of administration, therefore they do not have the powers of an executor.

It is important that the administrator does not intermeddle with the estate as otherwise he will not be able to renounce afterwards.

Certain basic activities such as insuring the property and feeding animals would be regarded as necessary and not intermeddling.

<u>Vesting</u>

Property vests in the executor immediately but not with the administrator.

Obviously on the sale of property such as land the purchaser will expect to see the grant of probate even though it automatically vests in the executor.

Ascertaining the assets and liabilities.

<u>Good practice is to use a checklist and examples as follows:</u>

1.   Will

Where kept

Letter of Authority to release

Name & Address of Executors

1) ....

       2).......................................

....

....

.

3) ....

       4).......................................

....

.

....

.

1. No Will

Entitlement to estate..

Name & Address of Administrators

1)

....

....

....

2. Particulars of Deceased

Full
Name...

Alias..

Date of Death   ....   Dateof Birth..............

Last Usual Address..

Married Status: Married / Single / Divorced / Widowed

Occupation...

Surviving Relatives:

Spouse [] Children [   ] Parents [   ]

Domicile:

England & Wales   [   ] Scotland [   ]

Wales   [   ]

National Insurance

Number...

Accountant:

Name...

Address...

Stockbroker / Financial Advisor

Name...

Address...

Bank Details

Name   ....   Account no.........

Address..

<u>Joint Property</u>

Asset:

House   [   ] Bank a/c   [   ] Investments [   ]

Description...

Joint
Holder..

Joint Tenants   [   ]   Tenants in Common   [

Schedule of assets and debts

Asset	Probate Value £	Corrected Value £	Grant Registered	Proceeds £
Stocks Shares				
National Savings Certificates				
Building Society a/c				
Current a/c Bank				
Deposit a/c Bank				
Premium Bonds				
Life Policies Bonds				
Freehold Property				
Leasehold Property				

Debts

Creditor Name	Nature of Debt	Amount £	Corrected Amount £	Date Paid
Utilities				
Inland Revenue				
Funeral A/c				

This checklist can immediately form the basis of the estate account and can be split into assets and liabilities.

VALUING THE ESTATE

Letters should be sent to all holders of assets that need valuation

The letter should ask

1. Details of the asset i.e. how much is in the account.

2. Any income that has accrued since death such as interest.

3. Send a copy of the death certificate as banks will normally expect to see this.

4. Ask for any forms which may become necessary to sell or close the account for signature by the executors after the grant of probate.

Bank and building society accounts

You will need to ask the following

1.   Balance plus interest if any

2.   Details of any other accounts

3.   Any items held on safe deposit.

4.   Details of any standing orders or any money received after date of death which may need to be refunded such as pension payments.

5.   You may need to borrow the IHT liability so ask them for any details that they might want.

Banks and building societies are more liberal about this and it is better to ask for money in the existing account if this is possible. If not a loan will need to be set up.

Stocks and shares

A list of all the shares should be set up.

You need to be meticulous with the actual share certificates that you take possession of. Make sure you create a schedule and get the executors or informants to sign the list by way of confirmation that is all they have given you.

People are exceedingly lax with certificates. And arguments can arise later as to what originals you possess

Obtain valuation from a stockbroker for which a fee is payable. Take instructions from the beneficiaries if at some date they wish them to be sold.

National Savings

Make application to the Director of Savings to obtain a valuation and forms to cash the holdings if necessary.

Building society accounts

Similar letter as to bank.

Social security /Pension

Letter to local office ask for balances or amounts owed.

Private Pension scheme

As above

Life Assurance

Obtain value of policy

Obtain Claim form

Land

An estate agent's valuation. Unless it is a farm then a full professional valuation as you may be claiming a relief.

It is possible for the executors to give a valuation but the district valuer will be keen to be involved. Also you need to be aware that for Capital Gains Tax purposes that the value at death will be the start value for the beneficiaries if the property is sold at a later date or transferred by way of assent. It is therefore important to get this right even if no IHT is payable. It will be much more difficult many years later to do a back calculation. Remind beneficiaries of this so that you are not involved in hours of abortive work at some future date.

Funeral expenses

It is good practice to ask the holders of any funds to pay the funeral account. This has a double effect. It removes any embarrassment by the beneficiaries as the funeral director may contact them. It helps the funeral directors cash flow and cuts down any further administration by you.

Council Tax

There will be an exemption so write to the council immediately if the property is empty.

All other debts

Write and ask for accounts and state you will pay them once probate has been granted and the funds are available.

HM Customs and Excise

If the deceased had an accountant supply him with a copy of death certificate and ask for his requirements.

Statutory advertisements

By advertising a personal representative will discharge his duty for payment of accounts not known by him.

Searches

Should you do a bankruptcy search against the deceased? Similarly you may wish to take a bankruptcy search against any large beneficiaries as if you pay them the money and not their trustee in bankruptcy you may not have discharged your duty.

The Executors may be liable if property / money is handed to someone who is bankrupt. They cannot give a valid receipt

Taxation of the Estate
There are three taxes that could affect the estate.

1. Income Tax
2. Capital Gains Tax
3. Inheritance Tax

The personal representatives are under a duty to deal with the deceased's tax affairs, and settle any outstanding liabilities and claim any rebates that may be necessary.

If the estate is large enough they will have to complete and submit the Inheritance Tax Account before probate or Letters of Administration will be granted.

In the event of inheritance tax having to be paid this will have to be paid before the grant is made.

Income tax

A return must be made to HMRC with the deceased's income up to the date of the death. The personal representative therefore should write to HMRC firstly to report the death and secondly to obtain a return to discover whether any tax may be due or owed to the estate.

The estate is entitled to the full personal reliefs for the tax year in question regarding the death.

Income received

Income received during the administration period.

There may be income that is being received during the administration period, such as salary, rent, dividends and interest on any investments.

Estate Income

This is income received during the administration period and finishes on the day when the value of the residuary estate is calculated for distribution purposes.

The personal representative must pay income tax received during the administration period although there are no personal reliefs.

The only advantage is that the estate in not liable for a higher rate tax which is currently 40%. There is relief for any interest paid, and may arise as a result of obtaining allowance for the inheritance tax.

Capital Gains Tax

The personal representatives must settle any Capital gains tax payable on any gains made during the deceased's lifetime. There is no Capital gains tax liability just as a result of the death and the personal representatives and beneficiaries ultimately are treated as acquiring the assets on the deceased's death, at their market value at the date of death.

It can therefore be very important to have a correct valuation of assets even though inheritance tax may not be payable, this will be the starting point for the beneficiaries in any future capital gains tax liability.

Inheritance Tax

Inheritance tax is payable on the value of all the property that the deceased owned, up to the date of death. This includes property passing under his will, or under the intestacy rules as well as property held under a joint tenancy and nominated property. There are important exemptions, depending on who is the beneficiary, and no inheritance tax will be payable in the following circumstances.

- Spouse of a deceased
- A Charity
- A Political party
- Some national bodies such as museums and art galleries

Inheritance tax may be avoided is there is business property or agricultural property relief and inheritance tax may be payable if the deceased has died within seven years of making a lifetime gift. There is however tapering relief over the seven year period.

As we have discussed, the Chancellor has announced, in the July 2015 budget, that he is increasing the IHT allowance to £1m (for a couple) for the family home. People will not have to pay IHT on properties worth less than £1million. This will be phased in from April 2017. However, there are a few things to note. The 'Family Homes Allowance' will apply only to property left to direct descendants, children, grandchildren, great grandchildren and so on. Stepchildren will also count. The allowance will not apply to indirect descendants such as nieces and nephews. It is also suggested that advice should be sought when thinking of downsizing as the new IHT rules may affect your tax liabilities.

Raising funds for paying the IHT on the personality

It is possible to pay instalments on land but not on the personal possessions. This has to be paid before the grant is made so you may have to borrow the tax before you have access to the funds.

Once borrowed or accessed the cheque will usually be in favour of HMRC.

Building Societies

This could be your best source of funds as they may allow you to have a cheque with only forms signed by the executors.

Direct Payment Scheme

Banks are now more susceptible to paying the money direct to HMRC which is only fair as it is the deceased's money and therefore the estates.

Beneficiary

Some beneficiaries may be able to pay IHT out of their own resources so as not to incur interest. Please ask.

****

4

MAKING THE APPLICATION-AFTER THE GRANT

The grant of representation is the official document issued by the court and is conclusive proof that the administrators or executors legal authority to deal with the estate.

<u>Registration</u>

The form for application for probate is form PA1. (In Scotland it is form C1 applying for confirmation). When making an application for probate you need to state how many office copies you require. At £215 pounds (2015/16) for the Grant and 50pence each sealed office copy you should obtain enough for you to send copies to collect in the estate expeditiously. There is no fee if the estate is under £5,000.

If you need help with the process of applying for probate or advice on inheritance tax you should call the Probate and Inheritance Tax helpline on 0300 123 1072. Probate forms should be sent to your local Probate Registry. You can find out details by contacting:

HM Revenue and Customs - Trusts and Estates, Inheritance Tax
Ferrers House
Castle Meadow Road
Nottingham
NG2 1BB
United Kingdom

Swear an oath

The probate office will send you an oath and details of how to arrange an appointment. You'll need to swear the oath at either:

- the office of a commissioner for oaths (usually a solicitor)

- a local probate office

The oath is a promise that the information you've given is true to the best of your knowledge.

You should get the grant through the post within 10 working days of swearing the oath.

If it's not possible to issue a grant, the Probate Service will explain why in writing.

Once you have the grant of probate it is good practice to send a photocopy to the executors/ beneficiaries to prove you have probate. Make it clear it is not an office copy as otherwise they will start using it for their own purposes and will be very disappointed when they get turned down by banks etc.

Whilst registering the grant you should send any claim form along so as to transfer withdraw or sell the assets. These should have been signed in readiness by the executors.

Deposit

As money comes in over and above what you need to settle immediate debts you should be putting the funds on deposit. If in a separate interest bearing account this will assist as you will not have to calculate the interest payable if it has been on deposit throughout the administration.

Realising the Assets

The most urgent matter may be paying off the IHT loan

Clearing the tax liabilities

Complete the tax return form R27 or R40 You should complete the tax return form for the period from the previous 6 April to the date of death.

Clearing the IHT position

The personal representatives may have given their own estimate of the value. As previously mentioned this value could have an effect on future tax for the beneficiaries Capital gains tax purposes. If the property is well below the IHT limit then the value of the land should be put in at as high a valuation as possible.

If the property that is subject to IHT is sold later for a lower figure than the probate value agreed then, if within three years of the date of death, you will be able to claim IHT loss relief.

Payment on account

If you have elected to pay by instalments, the instalment within six months after the end of the month on which the death occurred any tax outstanding is subject to interest.

Corrective account

If there is any variation on the agreed figures after the estate has been settled then a corrective account can be submitted for an overpayment or underpayment. If only minor then it may be acceptable to do this by letter and an assessment will be issued.

Clearance certificate.

Once all IHT has been paid and before final distribution you should obtain a clearance certificate form the capital taxes Offices on an IHT30. This will give the personal perspectives protection against any further claims.

If further assets become available obviously they should be declared

Instalment Option - Property

The personal representatives may elect to pay tax by instalments of up to ten equal instalments per year over ten years on land, certain securities and businesses.

Capital Gains tax

No charge to capital Gains tax arises on death. The assets are deemed to have been acquired at their market value at that date. When the asset is transferred to the beneficiaries they are deemed to have acquired the assets at the value at death. If there is a chargeable gain during the administration after claiming their allowances it will be subject to 40 per cent tax.

HMRC Charge

Whilst there is tax outstanding HMRC have a charge against those assets.

Distribution of the estate

EXECUTOR'S YEAR-Personal representatives have a year from the date of death before the beneficiaries can call upon them to distribute any part of the estate this is called the executors' year.

Personal representatives should protect themselves before distributing the estate.

The problems that could arise are an Outstanding tax liabilities this could include IHT, CGT and Income Tax. Obtain clearance certificates for all those:

Outstanding Debts

Place statutory advert if in doubt. Ones to look out for are funeral expenses and the headstone which may be placed later.

Unknown beneficiaries

Such as all the grandchildren these include both legitimate and illegitimate relatives.

Rectification action

There is a possibility that the will might be rectified within the first six months. Any action after six months requires leave of the court and the personal representatives are protected.

Family provision claims

Again if within the six months there may be a family provision claim.

Variation or disclaimer

Any deed of family arrangement could mean that a beneficiary will not accept a gift and disclaimer cannot be made once a beneficiary has accepted the gift.

Specific Problems - Dead Beneficiaries

If a beneficiary has died before the testator prima facie the gift will lapse unless the gift was of the whole or part of the residue in which case it will pass on to the person's estate.

Bankrupt beneficiaries.

It might be good practice to search against the beneficiaries as if any gift should be paid to the trustee in bankruptcy, the personal representatives need a valid receipt.

Which property pays the tax?

The Will should provide this

Specific Gift

This will entitle the beneficiary to all income and interest on that item since death it still does not become the property of the beneficiary until it has been vested in them

Assents of land.

This transfers the land to the beneficiaries. Now an AS1

Although no stamp duty you still have to complete an SDLT form.

Memorandum of the assent should be endorsed on the probate. This is obviously not so important now that land is registered as it would be difficult to try and transfer the same piece of land twice without becoming immediately aware of it!

FORMALITIES TO TRANSFER VARIOUS ASSETS

Personal chattels etc

By delivery no set method may be by conduct writing or verbally.

Bank account

Written instructions to bank or by cheque to beneficiary

National savings certificate etc

Withdrawal forms

Stocks and shares

Share or stock transfer forms.

Registered/Unregistered land

AS1

****

Schedule of Standard Probate Letters

(See overleaf)

1.   Letter to Debtors

2.   Letter to Creditors

3.   Letter to Bank applying for payment of Funeral Account

4.   Letter to Bank applying for payment of Inheritance Tax

5.   Letter to Capital Taxes re Inheritance Tax

6.   Letter to Probate Registry for Grant of Probate

7.   Letter to Bank or Building Society collecting funds

8.   Authority for receiving money

9.   Letter to Registrar to transfer shares

10.   Letter paying bills from the Estate

11.   Letter to Beneficiaries with statement for approval

12.   Letter sending Pecuniary Legacy

13.   Receipt for Pecuniary Legacy *(on behalf of ....)*

14.   Receipt for Pecuniary Legacy

15.   Letter to Beneficiary

16.   Receipt for Beneficiary

17.   Instruction sheet for a Will

STANDARD LETTERS

Please note that these are for guidance only and may change depending on the circumstances.

1. <u>Letter to Debtors</u>

Any date

Address

Dear Sirs

Re *Name – deceased*
Description
Account No:

We enclose certified copy of the Death Certificate of the above and should be obliged if you would let us know the amount outstanding to the credit of this account including interest accrued but not credited at the date of death.

Probate will be registered with you in due course.

If you have any form or if you require authority for the Executors to sign to let us have any proceeds, repayments or monies due to the Estate could you please let us have such forms.

Alternatively please confirm at this stage exactly what authority you will require. This should save delays once Probate has been granted.

Yours faithfully

2.   Letter to Creditors

Any date

Customer Services
Address

Dear Sirs

Re *Name* – **deceased**
Account Number:

We act on behalf of the Estate of the above unfortunately
……….. died on the
…………….. we enclose a copy of the death certificate for your information and retention.

We would be obliged if you would kindly forward all future accounts to ourselves. We are currently making application for Probate, once this is available we will pay all outstanding accounts.

Yours faithfully

3. Letter to Bank Applying for Payment of Funeral Account

Any date

Bank/Building Society
Address

Dear Sirs

Re *Name*   —   **deceased**
      Address:
      Account No:

As you are aware we act on behalf of the Estate of the Late
....

We enclose a copy of the funeral account and we would be obliged if it is at all possible for you to draw a cheque in favour of .... to pay this account. If you require any forms to be signed by our client please do not hesitate to contact us.

Your assistance is appreciated

Yours faithfully

4.   Letter to Bank applying for payment of Inheritance Tax

Any date

Bank
Address

Dear Sirs

Re   ....   –   **deceased**
Account No: ....

As you are aware we act for the Estate of the Late
....

There is a small amount of £........... due for Inheritance Tax and we would be obliged if it is at all possible for you to draw a cheque in favour of Her Majesty's Revenue and Customs to pay the amount due.

If you require any forms to be signed by the Executors please do not hesitate to contact us.

Your assistance is appreciated.

Yours faithfully

5.   Letter to Capital Taxes re Inheritance Tax

Any date

Capital Taxes Offices
Section K
Ferres House
PO Box 38
Castle Meadow Road
Nottingham NG2 1BB

Dear Sirs

Re   *Name* – deceased

We take this opportunity of enclosing the following:

1. A cheque in the sum of £??????? - the total amount of Inheritance Tax due

2. IHT200

3. D1

4. D7

5. D10

6. D13

7. D17

8. D18

We would be obliged if the D18 could be receipted and returned to us in due course.

Yours faithfully

6. Letter to Probate Registry for Grant of Probate

Any date

Ipswich District Probate Registry
8 Arcade Street
Ipswich
Suffolk IP1 1EJ

Dear Sirs

Re   Name – deceased

We enclose the following to lead to a Grant of Probate of the will of the above:

1. Oath for Executors

2. Will dated ?????

3. *Form IHT205 signed by the Executors*

    or

4. *D18*

5. Cheque in the sum of £????

We await hearing from you once Probate has been granted.

Yours faithfully

7. Letter to Bank or Building Society Collecting Funds

Any date
Bank/Building Society
Address

Dear Sirs

Re *Name*   **–**   **deceased**
      Account No: ....

We take this opportunity of enclosing the following:

1. Office Copy Probate – kindly return as soon as possible

2. Authority Letter/Withdrawal form

We await hearing from you with the proceeds of the account.

Yours faithfully

8.   Authority for Receiving Money

Any date

Bank plc
Address

Dear Sirs

Re   *Name*   –   deceased
Address
Account No: Sort   Code:
Account No: Sort Code:

We hereby give you authority to let .... of
.... have the proceeds due to the Estate of
the Late ....
Signature   ....
                       Name:

Signature   ....
                       Name:

Signature   ....
                       Name:

Dated   ....

9. Letter to Registrar to Transfer Shares

Any date

Registrars
Address

Dear Sirs

Re *Name* – **deceased**
.... **Shares**

We take this opportunity of enclosing the following:

1. Original Share Certificate

2. Stock Transfer Form duly signed by the Executors of the Estate

3. Office Copy Probate – Please return as soon as possible

We would be obliged if the Shares could be transferred into the name of ....

Kindly confirm to us when this has been completed.

Yours faithfully

10.   Letter paying bills from the Estate

Any date

Address

Dear Sirs

**Re   *Name*   –   deceased
Account Ref:**

We take this opportunity of enclosing your account together with a cheque in the sum of £..............

Kindly return your account duly receipted in due course and we would be obliged if you would kindly confirm that there are no further outstanding sums and this account is clear.

Yours faithfully

11.　　Letter to Beneficiary with Statement for Approval

Any date
Beneficiary Name
Address

Dear ....

Re　　*Name* **– deceased**

I take this opportunity of enclosing my statement of account. You will note that there is a retention of £............ which I will hold until I have confirmation that there are no further amounts due from the Estate.

If you would kindly confirm that the statement is in order I will arrange for your share of the residuary Estate to be paid to you immediately.

Yours sincerely

12.   Letter Sending Pecuniary Legacy

Any date *Address*

Dear ....

Re   *Name* **– deceased**
Address:

We act for the Estate of .... deceased. *Name of deceased* left you a legacy of £........... and we have pleasure in enclosing a cheque for that amount together with a receipt which please sign, date and return to me

Yours sincerely

13.   Receipt for Pecuniary Legacy *(on behalf of ....)*

IN THE ESTATE OF .... - DECEASED

I .... the Treasurer of
..............., *Address* acknowledge to have received from the
Executors of *Name* deceased the sum of .... Thousand
.... Hundred and .... Pounds (£.........) being the
pecuniary legacy bequeathed to the .... by his / her Will.

Dated   Any date

Signed ....

14. Receipt for Pecuniary Legacy

IN THE ESTATE OF .... - DECEASED

I .... acknowledge to have received from the Executors of .... deceased the sum of .... Thousand .... Hundred and .... Pounds and (£...............) being the pecuniary legacy bequeathed to me by his / her Will.

Dated   Any date

Signed ....

15.   Letter to Beneficiary

Any date

Address

Dear ....

Re *Name* **– deceased**

I take this opportunity of enclosing a cheque in the sum of £.......... which is the amount due to you as one of the beneficiaries of the Estate. *I am holding a small retention of £......... for ....*

I also enclose a copy of the statement for your information and a receipt which please sign, date and return to me

Yours sincerely

16. Receipt for Beneficiary

IN THE ESTATE OF .... - DECEASED

I .... acknowledge to have received from the Executors   of
.... deceased the sum of .... Pounds and .... Pence (£.................) being the share of the residuary Estate bequeathed to me by his / her Will.

Dated   Any date

Signed ....

17.   Instruction Sheet for a Will

Full Name: ....

Address: ....

....

Telephone No: ....

Executors: ....

Addresses: ....

Alternative Executors: ....

Addresses: ....

Beneficiaries: ....

....

Addresses: ....

....

(If the Beneficiaries are currently older than you, you may give consideration to appointing an alternative Beneficiary)

Alternative Beneficiaries: ....

Addresses ....

Any Specific Item you wish to give away: ....

....

Any Specific Sums of Money you wish to give away: ....

....

....

Any other wishes you may have (such as either being buried or cremated)

....

....

....

Signed: ....

Dated: ....

GLOSSARY OF TERMS

A

Abatement -When the Estate has insufficient money to pay the bills, then any gifts will be reduced pro rata to make enough money to pay such bills, debts and expenses.

Ademption-If when the Will comes into effect, that is the date of the death, the gift does not exist, the gift lapses. It may have been sold or given away during the deceased's lifetime.

Administrator/Administrix-In the event of an Intestacy, this is a definition of a person who deals with the deceased's estate.

Assent-A document which transfer the freehold or leasehold property to the beneficiary.

Assets-Everything belonging to the deceased

Attestation Clause-A note at the end of the Will, confirming that the Will has been properly signed and witnessed.

B

Bankruptcy-When a person cannot pay their debts, they can apply to the Court to have themselves made bankrupt or you can make someone else bankrupt if you are a creditor. The bankrupts' affairs are then run by the Trustee in bankruptcy until they are discharged.
Beneficiary

Bequeathed-Old fashioned word meaning – To leave someone property, more likely now to be bequest. A gift other than cash can be money or shares or other physical items.

Bona Vacantia-In the event of no other relative being alive, there is no one to inherit it goes to the Crown

C

Capacity-This means both mental and being of age that is 18 years old to be able to act as Executor or Administrator and a Beneficiary needs capacity to be able to receive the gift and give a valid receipt.

Capital Gains Tax (CGT)-When an asset has been owned during the deceased's lifetime and is sold for more than it was acquired for, then after deduction of allowances and reliefs, this tax is payable.

Caveat-A caution which will be given to the Probate Registry when there is doubt about the validity of the Will or whether there is a dispute about who is entitled to be the Executor.

Chargeable Gift-Anything left under the terms of the Will or during a person's lifetime, which is liable to tax.

Chattels-These are such things as pets, cars, boats, furniture, jewellery ornaments etc. Business assets money and securities are not chattels.

Children-The covers both legitimate and illegitimate children together with legally adopted children. This does not include stepchildren.

Codicil-An additional Will to make changes in your original Will.

Contentious Probate-Where someone lodges a caveat preventing the issue of a grant and their objections over such matters as the validity of the Will or the entitlement of someone to apply for the grant.

Continent Gift-Something left with a condition attached, which is an age or a condition.

Conveyancing-The process by which land and buildings are transferred.

Court of Protection-Any Power of Attorney either registered or unregistered or the persons affairs were with the Receivers then all such powers lapse on death.

D

Death Certificate-When a death is registered you should obtain extra copies for anyone who needs them. Most institutions want to see the original copy, not a photocopy.

Devise-Old fashioned word meaning to give

Deeds of Variation-If all the beneficiaries agree, then after the death, the terms of the Will may be altered, usually for the purpose of saving Inheritance Tax. It has to be drawn up within two years of the date of death.

Distribution of the Estate-Once probate has been granted, and all monies have been collected it, all debts and taxes have been paid and the accounts agreed, then the Estate may be distributed.

Donation of Organs-The deceased may give directions for the disposal of their body. The decision is that of the Executors who will generally follow the wishes of the deceased

E

Enduring Power of Attorney (EPOA)-If an Enduring Power of Attorney was being used prior to death this will cease on death.

Engrossment-A final copy of a document.

Excepted Estate-These are estates under a certain limit that do not have to be notified to the Inland Revenue

Executor/Executrix-The Person named in the Will to deal with the deceased Estate.

G

Grant of Letter of Administration-This means the dealing with the deceased's Estate after death. The administration is undertaken by an Administrator, if there is no Will or an Executor if there is a Will.

Grant of Probate-This is where there is a Will and an Executor has been appointed.

Guardians-People appointed by the Will, another parent or the Court to act with parental responsibility for a child.

H

Half Blood-Where people share only one parent in common, they are of the half blood. For example Brother of the half blood.

Headstones-Reasonable costs of the headstone can be deducted with the funeral from the Estate together with reasonable cost of the wake. Again, depending on the size of the Estate.

I

IHT-Inheritance Tax

Intestacy-Where no Will has been made

Intestate-The person who Dies without making a Will

Issue-Or living descendant

J

Joint Tenant-Usually the surviving spouse and the property automatically passes to the surviving spouse and there is an Inheritance Tax exemption.

Joint Assets-Two or more persons have a legal interest in a property, usually land and buildings. Normally, all the other joint owners inherit automatically. They are assessed for Inheritance Tax purposes, even though they pass automatically to the surviving joint owners. A proper valuation should be made.

L

Land Registry-Land Registry www.landreg.gov.uk.

Leasehold property-The Executor/Administrator retains any rights that the original Leaseholder would have had, such as being able to buy the freehold etc.

Legacy-A gift left to someone in a Will other than house or land.

Letter of Administration-Equivalent to the Grant of Probate where no Will has been made

Liabilities-Another word for debts. They need to be identified and show in any probate application. Any creditors will need to be informed and once funds have been gathered these debts should be paid off.

Life Interest-The right to enjoy the benefit for life.

M-Minor/Infant-Any child under the age of 18

N

Newspaper Advertisements-These involve Obituary Notices and Trustee Act Notices

O

Oath-An oath is a sworn statement, usually whilst holding the Bible but an affirmation of the truth can be made instead of swearing on the Bible.

Office Copy Entries-This is evidence of the property title at the Land Registry.

P

Pecuniary Legacy-Any Specific amount of money

Personal Representative-Can mean either the Executor or Administrator, just a general term to cover them both.

Probate-Confirmation that the Will is valid and the Executors have the authority to deal with the Estate

R

Renunciation-The Executor has the right to renounce, which means giving up his or her right to be the Executor. To renounce the Executor needs to sign a Form or Letter of Renunciation, which is then sent to the Probate Registry by the proving Executor

Residue-This is the Estate of the deceased, which remains after distribution to the beneficiaries after payment of all gifts and all taxes, debts etc.

Revocation of Will-This means to cancel any previously written Will. Usually a new Will will revoke a previously written Will or it can be revoked in other ways by destroying it etc.

s

Small Estate-Any Estate under the figure of £5000.00

Specific Legacy-A gift of some specific item such as a physical item – car or an amount of money

Spouse-Old legal term for a Wife or Husband.

Survivorship-Where two or more joint Tenants have outlived the deceased. The joint Tenant then inherits a share of the Estate automatically by survivorship. No probate needs to be proved.

T

Tenant-Either a joint tenant or tenant in common. Confusing to the public as this is nothing to do with leasehold property. Therefore you can be a joint tenant or tenant in common of freehold property.

Tenants in common-This is where property is held by two or more people in different shares. Unless shown otherwise, it will usually be fifty/fifty like joint tenants. If one Tenant dies their share passes according to the Will.

Testamentary expenses-Reasonable costs incurred in the administration of the estate. Professional Executors are unable to receive compensation unless it is specific term of the Will.

Testator/Testatrix-This is a person making the Will. Testatrix is the female form.

Trust-An arrangement to hold property for another. The Trustee is not the legal owner.

Trustees-This is where somebody who is responsible to hold Trust assets on behalf of the beneficiaries.

U

Unregistered Land-Certain areas of land have not been registered as there has been no transfer or other variation of the Title. This is equally as affective as registered land but the Land Registry are changing the rules so within the foreseeable future, all land will become registered.

Undue Influence-Where pressure either mental or physical will be put on a party to do an act against their will.

V

Validity of Will-For a Will to be valid it has to be in writing, signed, witnessed correctly and the Testator has to know he or she is signing.

W

Will

****

Useful Addresses

Department for National Savings

Glasgow G58 1SB
For enquiries about Capital Bonds, Childrens Bonus Bonds, FIRST Option Bonds, Fixed Rate Savings Bonds, Ordinary Accounts and Investment Accounts.
www.nsandi.com
Tel: 0500 007 007

Department of Work and Pensions
Caxton House
Tothill Street
London
SW1H 9NA
www.dwpguide.co.uk
Tel: 0843 116 0031

HM Revenue and Customs Capital Taxes Office
Tel: 0300 123 1072

The Law Society of England and Wales
www.lawsociety.org.uk

London Gazette
PO Box 3548
Norwich NR7 7WD
0333 200 2434 www.thegazette.co.uk

Solicitors Regulation Authority
The Cube
199 Wharfside Street
Birmingham
B1 1RN
www.sra.org.uk
0370 606 2555
Information on solicitors specialising in wills and probate

The Principal Probate Registry
First Avenue House
42-49 High Holborn
London WC1V 6NP
Probate Helpline 0300 123 1072
Enquiries 0207 421 8509

Useful Addresses in Scotland
Accountant of Court
2 Parliament Square
Edinburgh EH1 1RQ
0131 240 6742
www.scotscourts.gov.uk

Law Society of Scotland

26 Drumsheugh Gardens
Edinburgh
EH3 7YR
0131 226 7411 www.lawscot.org.uk

Registers of Scotland
Customer Service Centre

Meadowbank House
153 London Road
Edinburgh
HE8 7AU
0800 169 9391
(Head Office)

Or

Registers of Scotland
Hanover House
24 Douglas Street
Glasgow
G2 7NQ
0800 169 9291
www.ros.gov.uk

Sheriff Clerks Office
Commissary Department
27 Chambers Street
Edinburgh EH1 1LB
0131 225 2525

****

Index

****

Schedule of Probate Forms

1. IHT205 – Return of Estate Information
2. IHT400 – Inland Revenue Account for Inheritance Tax
3. IHTWS – Inheritance Tax work sheet
4. Oath for Executors
5. Oath for Administrators
6. Stock / Share Transfer Form
7. AS1

The Following Probate Forms, which are shown overleaf, are obtainable on the website:

www.HMCourt-service.gov-uk.
www.probate.co.uk/advice.

8.	PA5	- Do I need a grant of representation?
9.	N205D	– Notice of issue (Probate Claim)
10.	PA1	- How to obtain Probate
11.	PA1A	- Guidance notes for Probate Application
11.	PA1S	- Application for Probate Search
12.	PA2	-How to obtain Probate guide for the applicant without solicitor
13.	PA3	– Probate fees
14.	PA4	- Directory of Probate Registries and interview venues

****

Do I need a grant of representation (probate or letters of administration)?

A guide for people dealing with the estate when someone has recently died

What is the Probate Service?

The Probate Service is part of HM Courts & Tribunals Service. It administers the system of probate, which gives people the legal right to handle the estate (for example, money, possessions and property) of a deceased person.

This leaflet is to advise you whether you need a Grant of Representation to obtain probate when someone has died.

If you have any queries, please contact your local Probate Registry. The staff are there to help you – but they cannot give you legal advice.

Introduction

When a person dies, they usually leave an estate (including money, possessions and property) and sometimes a will.

Any will names one or more executors to be responsible for collecting in all the money, paying any debts and distributing any legacies left to individuals or organisations.

In order to access the estate, the executor needs to apply to the Probate Registry for a document called a Grant of Representation or 'grant'. This process is called probate. The grant establishes who can legally collect money from banks, building societies and other organisations which hold assets belonging to the deceased person.

In most cases, applying for probate is a straightforward procedure. The Probate Registry administers applications for grants throughout England and Wales.

The information in this leaflet refers only to the law in England and Wales. If the deceased person was domiciled in Scotland, Northern Ireland or another country when they died, you will need to contact the court in the appropriate country.

How do I know if a grant is needed?

Not every estate needs a grant. A grant may not be needed if:

- The home is held in joint names and is passing by survivorship to the other joint owner(s). This is usually the case for married couples and those in a legal civil partnership.

- There is a joint bank or building society account. In this case, the bank may only need to see the death certificate, in order to arrange for the money to be transferred to the other joint owner. However, a grant may still be needed to access assets held in other bank accounts or insurance policies.

  The amount held in each account was very small. You will need to check with the organisations (banks, building societies or insurance companies) involved to find out if they will release the assets without a grant.

If none of the circumstances above apply, a grant will be required.

Who should apply for the grant?

Usually, the will names executor(s) to administer the estate and apply for the grant. If there is no executor or there is no will, the direct next of kin will usually apply.

If a number of family members are named in the will, you can decide between you who should apply. More than one person can apply.

Whoever applies needs to be over 18 and should be prepared to take on the role of collecting money from banks, building societies and other organisations and transferring it to the people named in the will.

How do I apply for the grant?

You can find out how to do this in leaflet **PA2 'How to obtain probate'**, which is available on our website.

You can also contact the Probate and Inheritance Tax Helpline 0845 3020900.

Alternatively, you can consult a solicitor, who will be able to advise you.

Useful contacts

For general information on wills and probate:
www.direct.gov.uk/en/RightsAndResponsibilities/Death/index.htm

For information about the Probate Service and online forms:
http://www.hmcourts-service.gov.uk/infoabout/civil/probate/index.htm

To find out addresses of regional probate registries:
http://www.hmcourts-service.gov.uk/infoabout/civil/probate/registries.htm

For information about Inheritance Tax and online forms:
www.hmrc.gov.uk/cto

For more detailed information about probate and Inheritance Tax or to obtain application forms contact:
Probate and Inheritance Tax Helpline: 0845 3020900

Probate forms and leaflets

PA1   Probate application form

PA1A   Probate application form (guidance notes)

PA2   How to obtain probate (leaflet)

PA3   Probate fees list (leaflet)

PA4   Directory of probate registries and interview venues (leaflet)

PA5   Do I need a grant of representation (probate or letters of administration)? (leaflet)

PA6   What will happen at my probate interview? (leaflet)

PA7   How to deposit a will with the Probate Service (leaflet)

PA7A   Withdrawing your will from the Principal Probate Registry (form)

PA8   How to enter a caveat (leaflet)

PA8A   How to enter a caveat (form)

PA9   How to enter a general search (leaflet)

PA10   How to enter a standing search (leaflet)

PA1S   Application for a probate search (form)

HMRC Inheritance Tax forms

IHT205 Return of estate information

IHT206 Return of estate information (guidance notes)

IHT400 Inheritance Tax Account

tice of issue
obate claim)

In the

Claim No.

Claimant(s)

Defendant(s)

Issue fee

e estate of   deceased (Probate)

claim was issued on [   ]

court sent it to the defendant(s) by first class post on [   ]

it will be deemed served on [   ]].

claim form (which includes particulars of claim) is returned to you, with the relevant response forms, for

to serve them on the defendant(s)]

es for guidance

claim form and particulars of claim, if served separately, must be served on the defendant within 4 months e date of issue (6 months if you are serving outside England and Wales). You may be able to apply to nd the time for serving the claim form but the application must generally be made before the 4 month or onth period expires.

must inform the court immediately if your claim is settled.

defendant must file an acknowledgment of service and defence within 28 days of service of the Particulars Claim (whether they are served with the claim form or separately). A longer period applies if the defendant rved outside England and Wales.

ault judgment **cannot** be obtained in a probate claim.

o defendant acknowledges service or files a defence, and the time for doing so has expired, you may apply to court for an order that the claim proceed to trial.

To

Ref.

5D Notice of issue (probate) (10.01)

Probate Application Form - PA1

Please use **BLOCK CAPITALS**

Name of deceased	
Interview venue	*(see PA4)*
Dates to avoid	

Please read the following questions and PA2 booklet 'How to obtain probate' carefully before filling in this form. Please also refer to the Guidance Notes PA1a where an item is marked *.

PLEASE COMPLETE ALL SECTIONS.

This column is for official use

Section A: The Will / Codicil

*A1 Did the deceased leave a will/codicil? *(Note: These may not necessarily be formal documents. If the answer to question 1 is Yes, you must enclose the **original** document(s) with your application.)*

Will		Codicil
Yes ☐ No ☐		Yes ☐

If **No** to both questions, please go to Section B

Date of will

Date of codicil

A2 Did the deceased marry or enter into a Civil Partnership after the date of the will/codicil?
Yes ☐ Date: No ☐

A3 Is there anyone under 18 years old who receives anything in the will/codicil?
Yes ☐ No ☐

A4 Did any of the witnesses to the will or codicil or the spouse/civil partner of any witness receive a gift under the will/codicil? If Yes, state name of witness.
Yes ☐ No ☐

A5 Are there any executors named in the will/codicil?
Yes ☐ No ☐

A = Pre-deceased
B = Died after the deceased
C = Power Reserved
D = Renunciation
E = Power of Attorney

*A6 Give the names of those executors who are **not** applying and the reasons why. **Note: All** executors **must** be accounted for.

Full names	Reason A,B,C,D,E

Section B: Relatives of the deceased

*B1 - B6

Please refer to the Guidance Notes.

Sections B1 - B4 must be completed in all cases.

Please state the **number** of relatives of the deceased in categories B1 - B4.

If there are no relatives in a particular category, write 'nil' in each box and move onto the next category.

Number of relatives (if none, write nil)	Under 18	Over 18
B1 Surviving **lawful** husband or wife or surviving **lawful** civil partner		
B2a Sons or daughters who survived the deceased		
b Sons or daughters who did **not** survive the deceased		
c Children of person(s) indicated at '**2b' only**, who survived the deceased *		
B3 Parents who survived the deceased		
B4a Brothers or sisters who survived the deceased		
b Brothers or sisters who did **not** survive the deceased		
c Children of person(s) indicated at '4b' **only**, who survived the deceased *		
B5 Grandparents who survived the deceased		
B6a Uncles or aunts who survived the deceased		
b Uncles or aunts who did **not** survive the deceased		
c Children of person(s) indicated at '6b' **only**, who survived the deceased *		

Note: Sections B5 and B6 only need to be completed if the deceased had no relatives in Section B1 - B4.

Section C: Details of applicant(s)

This column is for official use

Title   Mr ☐   Mrs ☐   Miss ☐   Ms ☐   Other ☐

Forenames

I.T.W.C

Surname

Address

Postcode:

Telephone number   Home

Work

E-mail address (optional)

Occupation

Are you related to the deceased?   Yes ☐   No ☐

If Yes, what is your relationship?   Relationship:

If there are any other applicants, up to a maximum of three, give their details. (Note: **All** applicants named in Sections C1 and C8 must attend an interview.)   Please give details below as C1 to C7 of other applicants who are entitled to apply and wish to be named in the grant.

Name and address of any surviving lawful husband or wife/civil partner of the deceased, unless stated above.

Postcode:

If you are applying as an attorney on behalf of the person entitled to the grant, please state their name, address and capacity in which they are entitled (e.g. relationship to the deceased).

Postcode:

Relationship:

a Has anyone been appointed by the person entitled as their attorney under an Enduring Power of Attorney (EPA) or a Property and financial affairs Lasting Power of Attorney (LPA)?   EPA ☐   LPA ☐   No ☐

b If Yes, has it been registered with the Office of the Public Guardian?   Yes ☐   No ☐

c Does the donor of the EPA/LPA lack mental capacity within the meaning of the Mental Capacity Act 2005? (see PA1a)   Yes ☐   No ☐

Section D: Details of the deceased

				This column is for official use
*D1	Forenames			
*D2	Surname			True name
*D3	Did the deceased hold any assets **(excluding joint assets)** in another name?	Yes ☐	No ☐	Alias
*D4a	If Yes, what are the assets?			
	And in what name(s) are they held?			Address
D4b	Was the deceased known by any other name in which he/she made a will? If so, what name was it made in?	Yes ☐	No ☐	
D5	Last permanent address of the deceased.			
		Postcode:		D/C district and No.
D6	Date of birth			
D7	Date of death	Age:		L.S.A.
*D8	**Domicile** Was England and Wales the domicile/permanent home of the deceased at the date of death? If No, please specify the deceased's permanent home or domicile.	Yes ☐	No ☐	D.B.F.

*D9 Tick the last **legal** marital or civil partnership status of the deceased, and give dates where appropriate.

Bachelor/Spinster	☐
Widow/Widower/Surviving Civil Partner	☐
Married/Civil Partnership	☐ Date:
Divorced/Civil Partnership dissolved	☐ Date:
Judicially separated	☐ Date:

Note: These documents (✦) may usually be obtained from the Court which processed the divorce/dissolution of civil partnership/separation.

*(If the deceased did **not** leave a will, please enclose official copy✦ of the Decree Absolute/Decree of Dissolution of Civil Partnership/Decree of Judicial Separation (as applicable))*

*D10	Was the deceased legally adopted?	Yes ☐	No ☐
*D11	Has any relative of the deceased been legally adopted? (If Yes, give name and relationship to deceased.)	Yes ☐	No ☐
	Name:		
	Relationship:		

D12 *Answer this section **only** if the deceased died before **4th April 1988** or left a will or codicil dated before that date.*

D12a	Was the deceased illegitimate?	Yes ☐	No ☐
D12b	Did the deceased leave any illegitimate sons or daughters?	Yes ☐	No ☐
D12c	Did the deceased have any illegitimate sons or daughters who died leaving children of their own?	Yes ☐	No ☐

Complete this section if you have filled in form IHT205(2011)/IHT207. You must file the form IHT205(2011)/IHT207 with your application.

If you have filled in a version of the IHT205(2011) or IHT205 dated before 1st January 2011 please ring the Helpline on 0300 123 1072 for advice.

I/we confirm that I/we have filled in form IHT205(2011)/IHT207 and I/we confirm that from the answers I/we have given on that form I/we are not required to fill in form IHT400 for this estate and the estate qualifies as an excepted estate. (Delete as applicable)

If you have filled in form IHT205(2011) –
Please transfer the following figures from form IHT205(2011) onto this form:

Figure from box D	£
Figure from box F	£
Figure from box H	£

If you have filled in form IHT207 –
Please transfer the following figures from form IHT207 onto this form:

Figure from box A	£
Figure from box C	£
Figure from box H	£

Complete this section if you have filled in form IHT400 and IHT421.

Please transfer the following figures from form IHT421 on to this form:

Gross value of assets (from Box 3 on the IHT421)	£
Net value (from Box 5 on the IHT421)	£

At the same time as sending the probate application forms to the probate registry you **must** also send the **IHT400** (and associated schedules and copy documents) and **IHT421** to:

HMRC, Inheritance Tax, Ferrers House, PO Box 38, Castle Meadow Road, Nottingham, NG2 1BB (DX701201 Nottingham 4)

When the tax has been paid or assessed to be an estate where tax is not payable HMRC will send the stamped IHT421 to the appropriate probate registry as you have indicated on the IHT421 form.

Section F: Submitting your application – **Important information**

Please send your application to the probate registry which controls the interview venue you wish to attend (see PA4) otherwise your application may be delayed.

You should send the following documents as applicable:

PA1

IHT205(2011)/IHT207/IHT217 signed by all applicants (see Section E i)
Note: Do not enclose IHT400 or IHT421 – these must be sent to HMRC (Inheritance Tax) (see Section E ii)

Original will and codicils plus three A4 sized photocopies of the will/codicil(s) (see separate notes)
Note: Do not remove or attach anything to the will/codicil

An official copy of any foreign will or any will dealing with assets abroad (and a translation if necessary)

Official copy of death certificate or coroner's letter – **not a photocopy**

Other documents as requested on PA1

Please state the number of official copy grants required to deal with assets **in** England and Wales (see PA3)	
Please state the number of official copy grants required to deal with assets **outside** England and Wales (see PA3)	
Please state total amount of cheque enclosed for fee (made payable to **HM Courts & Tribunals Service**) including cost for the number of official copy grants stated above (see PA3)	£

Dated

PLEASE ENSURE THAT ALL THE INFORMATION GIVEN IS ACCURATE AND THAT YOU KEEP COPIES OF ALL DOCUMENTS SENT. IF YOU DO NOT ENCLOSE ALL THE RELEVANT ITEMS YOUR APPLICATION MAY BE DELAYED.

Guidance Notes
for Probate Application Form PA1

These notes will help you to complete the parts of form PA1 marked *

Section A

A1 Please enclose the original will and any codicils with your application (**not** a photocopy).

A6 Please state the names of any executors named in the will who are not applying for the Grant of Probate and show one of the following reasons for this:-

A   The executor died before the deceased.

B   The executor died after the deceased.

C   The executor does not wish to apply for probate now but wishes to reserve the right to act as executor in the future if necessary – this option is referred to as having "power reserved".

D   The executor does not wish to apply for probate at all. This is referred to as "renouncing". It means that they gives up all their rights to act as executor.

E   The executor wants to appoint another person to act as their attorney to take the Grant of Representation out on their behalf. Please note, however, that the attorney of one executor cannot take a grant jointly with an executor acting in his own right.

If you give reason D or E, please send a letter signed by the executor stating their intention when you send the application to the Probate Registry. If option C, D, or E is stated the Probate Registry will, on receipt of your application, send you a form for the executor(s) to sign to confirm their intention. You should arrange for this to be completed and then return it to the Probate Registry as instructed.

Example for A6

A will appoints three executors – Brian Jones, Valerie Jones and Frank Smith. Brian Jones wishes to apply for the grant, Frank Smith dies before the deceased and Valerie Jones does not wish to apply for the grant at present, as she works full time and cannot attend the appointment. Valerie wishes to keep her options open however, just in case it becomes necessary for her to take out a Grant of Probate in future e.g. if Brian Jones dies before he has completed the administration. The form would be completed as follows:

Frank Smith	**A**
Valerie Jones	**C**

The Grant of Probate will issue to Brian Jones with "power reserved" to Valerie Jones. Valerie Jones will be asked to sign a "power reserved" form.

Section B

Sections B1 - B4 must be completed in all cases. Sections B5 - B6 only needs to be completed if the deceased had no relatives in Sections B1 - B4.

Note:

- This section refers to blood/legally adopted relatives only; details of step relatives are not required.
- The term "survived" means the person was alive when the deceased died.
- If the deceased had any half brothers or sisters/uncles/aunts (i.e. only one parent in common), please indicate this on the form.
- A civil partnership is defined as one between two people of the same sex which has been registered in accordance with the Civil Partnership Act 2004.

B2(c), B4(c) and B6(c)

B2(c) – Only include children of sons or daughters of the deceased entered in B2(b), where the children have survived the deceased.

B4(c) – Only include children of brothers or sisters of the deceased entered in B4(b), where the children have survived the deceased.

B6(c) – Only include children of uncles or aunts of the deceased entered in B6(b), where the children have survived the deceased.

© Crown Copyright 2008

If you are applying on behalf of the person entitled to the grant (i.e. as their attorney), you should send a letter signed by them confirming that they want you to apply with your application. If the person entitled to the grant has already signed an Enduring Power of Attorney (EPA), or a Property and financial affairs Lasting Power of Attorney (LPA) please send the original document to us. An LPA must be registered with the Office of the Public Guardian before it can be used. If the donor of the EPA or LPA is unable to make a decision for him/herself due to an impairment of or a disturbance in the functioning of the mind or brain (i.e. lacks capacity under the Mental Capacity Act (MCA) 2005) please contact us.

D1 - D2   Please state the full **true** name of the deceased. The true name usually consists of the forenames as shown on the person's birth certificate and the surname as shown on the death certificate. If this is not the case please contact us.

D3 - D4   If the deceased had any assets in any name(s) other than their true name these should be stated. You do not need to show here any assets held jointly with another person.

Example for D1 - D4:

Name on birth certificate	Emma Louise **Jones**
Name on death certificate	Emma Louise **Smith**

The deceased's true name is Emma Louise Smith.

The deceased had a bank account in the name of Louise Smith and was commonly known by this name. The form should be completed as follows:

Forenames	**Emma Louise**
Surname	Smith
Did the deceased hold any assets (excluding joint assets) in another name?	Yes
If yes, what are the assets?	Lloyds Bank Account
And in what name(s) are they held?	**Louise** Smith

The grant will issue in the name of "Emma Louise Smith otherwise known as Louise Smith".

D8   The domicile of the deceased at the date of their death must be established in each case. Generally a person is domiciled in the country which they consider to be their permanent home. However they may be domiciled in a country without having a permanent home there. If you are unsure what this means you should contact your local registry. You may need to seek legal advice regarding this.

D9   You do not initially need to supply a copy of the Decree Absolute, decree of dissolution of civil partnership or decree of Judicial Separation if the deceased left a will. However we may ask to see it later if necessary. You can obtain an official copy of these documents from the court that issued them or from Principal Registry of the Family Division, 42-49 High Holborn, London WC1V 6NP.

D10 - D11 If the deceased did **not** leave a will and the applicant for the grant is the adoptor/adoptee of the deceased, please file a copy of the entry in the Adopted Children's Register. An official copy of the entry in the Adopted Children's Register can be obtained from The General Register Office, Adoption Section, Smedley Hydro, Trafalgar Road, Birkdale, Southport PR8 2HH.

**If you have any general enquiries,
please telephone the Probate and Inheritance Tax Helpline
Telephone number: 0300 123 1072**

Application for a search (copies of grants and wills)

We offer two different types of searches, General Searches and Standing Searches. Please read the following guidance to help you determine what type of search you require and then complete the details overleaf.

General Search

A search of the probate records for England and Wales from 1858 to the present day.

A General Search is suitable when searching for information about an estate or for family history research and you wish to obtain a copy of the grant and will (if any) and additionally when you do not know the exact date of death.

Standing Search

An ongoing search that anticipates the issue of a grant and entitles you to a copy of the grant and will (if any) when it issues.

Your application is entered onto a database and remains in force for 6 months. The database matches the details you have sent to us to any grant, so to ensure a correct match please ensure the accuracy of the information supplied.

The date of death of the deceased **must** be within the last **six** months and you must supply the **exact** date of death.

If the date of death is **not** within the last six months you **must** have already carried out a general search which resulted in no record being found and you need to supply a copy of your No Trace letter with this application.

A Standing Search is suitable if you need to make a claim against an estate and need to know when the grant issues.

If you submit a Standing Search application that does not meet the above mandatory criteria then we will automatically conduct a General Search as standard.

Notes

- We aim to respond to all search requests within 21 working days **(four weeks)**.

  You will be sent:

  For a **General Search** either copies or a letter explaining there is no record of a grant in the estate.

  For a **Standing Search** an acknowledgment letter to confirm your Standing Search has been entered (including a reference number should you wish to extend it for a further 6 months) or if the grant has already issued, copies of the grant and will if applicable.

- If you require a General Search urgently for a Court hearing, property sale or other legal reason, please go in person to your local Probate Registry where, if Probate has been granted, copies can usually be provided within 24 hours. Please contact the registry prior to your visit as this service is not available at all registries.

- Any queries about submitted search applications **must be made in writing** to the address below. Please only write after four weeks have elapsed confirming when payment was taken.

- For further information on searches and copies please visit our website www.justice.gov.uk

Please complete **ALL** sections on the form overleaf and send it with your payment and any supporting documents to:

The Postal Searches and Copies Department, District Probate Registry,
York House, 31 York Place, Leeds, LS1 2BA

Please complete in CAPITAL LETTERS

Details of the deceased

Surname		Alternative spelling:
Forenames		Alternative spelling:
Address		
Date of death		(must be the exact date and within the last 6 months for a Standing Search)
Probate details (if known)	Grant type:	Issuing Registry:	Date:

Type of Search requested

Please tick the appropriate box (see guidance overleaf) and only tick one box.

General Search ☐   **Standing Search** (only for deaths in the last 6 months) ☐

If no box or both boxes are ticked a general search will be undertaken by default.

Document required/payment

Standing Searches

Fee payable for a Standing Search is £10 (must meet criteria overleaf for a Standing Search to be entered).

General Searches

Fee payable for a General Search including 1 copy of the grant and 1 copy of the will is £10.
As standard the copies are **not** sealed.

For General Searches **additional** copies of the grant are £0.50 each and the will £0.50 each.

In **TOTAL**, how many copies of:

the grant do you require? ☐

the will do you require? ☐

I enclose a cheque payable to 'HMCTS' to the value of £ ☐

For General Searches, **do not** tick this box unless you require the grant to administer the estate ☐

For General Searches, if you need the copies to administer the estate abroad please state the country/countries in which the deceased held assets in the box below:

Your details

Name/organisation	
Your reference (if any)	
Your postal address or DX number (if applicable)	

Please write the name of the deceased on the reverse of the cheque. If you are sending one cheque for multiple requests, one name on the cheque is sufficient.

How to obtain probate -

A guide for people acting without a solicitor

What is the Probate Service?

The Probate Service is part of HM Courts & Tribunals Service. It administers the system of probate in England and Wales, and issues grants of representation, which give people the legal right to handle the estate (for example, money, possessions and property) of a deceased person.

This leaflet provides guidance if you want to obtain probate without using a solicitor.

If you have any queries, please contact your local probate registry (see leaflet **PA4**). The staff are there to help you – but they cannot give you legal advice.

Introduction

When a person dies, they usually leave an estate (including money, possessions and property).

In order to access the estate, the personal representative(s) of the deceased need to apply to the Probate Service for a grant of representation (a grant). The grant establishes who can legally collect money from banks, building societies and other organisations which hold assets belonging to the deceased person.

In most cases, applying for a grant is a straightforward procedure. It will involve completing a form with supporting documents, and swearing an oath in support of the application.

The information in this leaflet refers only to the law in England and Wales. If the deceased person was permanently resident in any other country when they died, please contact your nearest probate registry for guidance.

What is the purpose of the grant of representation?

A grant establishes who can legally collect money from banks, building societies and other organisations which hold assets belonging to the deceased person. There are three types of grant:

Probate

Probate is issued by the Probate Service to the executor(s) named in a will left by the deceased.

Letters of Administration (with will)

Letters of Administration (with will) are issued when no executor is named in the will, or when the executors are unable or unwilling to apply for the grant.

Letters of Administration

Letters of Administration are issued when the deceased person has not made a will, or the will they have made is not valid.

Is a grant always needed?

Not every estate needs a grant. A grant may not be needed if:

- the home is held in joint names and is passing by survivorship to the other joint owner(s).
- there is a joint bank or building society account. In this case, the bank may only need to see the death certificate, in order to arrange for the money to be transferred solely to the other joint owner. However, a grant could still be needed to access assets held in accounts not held in joint names, or insurance policies.
- the amount held in each account was small (even if held in the deceased's sole name). You will need to check with the organisations (banks, building societies or insurance companies) involved to find out if they will release the assets without a grant.

You may wish to ask anyone holding the deceased's money (such as a bank or insurance company) whether they will release it to you without seeing a grant. If they agree, they may attach conditions such as asking you to sign a statutory declaration before a solicitor. You will then be able to decide whether it is cheaper or easier to do this than to apply for a grant.

Please note that a grant **must** be presented in order to sell or transfer a property held in the deceased's sole name or a share of a property held jointly with the deceased and one or more other people as tenants-in-common. Tenancy-in-common is a written agreement between two or more people who own a joint asset (usually land or buildings). If you aren't sure about this you may wish to consult a solicitor.

You cannot complete a sale on any property owned, or partly owned, by a deceased person until the grant has been issued. It is therefore advisable not to put properties owned, or partly owned by the deceased, up for sale until a grant has been issued.

Who can apply for probate?

You can apply for a grant if you are over the age of 18 and:

- you are an executor named in the will;
- you are named in the will to receive some or all of the estate (if there are no executors, or if the executors are unable or unwilling to apply); or

- the deceased person did not make a will and you are their next of kin, in the following order of priority:

  - lawful husband or wife or civil partner (a civil partnership is defined as a partnership between two people of the same sex which has been registered in accordance with the Civil Partnership Act 2004). The surviving partner of co-habiting couples not in a marriage or civil partnership are not entitled to apply for a grant.

  - sons or daughters (excluding step-children) including children adopted by the deceased. (Children adopted out of their biological family can only apply in the estates of their adoptive parents and not their biological parents.)

  - parents

  - brothers or sisters

  - grandparents

  - uncles or aunts

  - If sons, daughters, brothers, sisters, uncles or aunts of the deceased person have died before the deceased, their children may apply for a grant.

Usually, only one of the personal representatives is required to apply for a grant. However, if the person entitled to the estate is under 18, two people are legally required to apply for a grant. If this is the case we will let you know when we receive your application.

When more than one person wants to apply for a grant, they may make a joint application. A maximum of four applicants is allowed and they will all have to swear an oath in support of their application.

When you submit your application we will check to ensure that the right person(s) are applying for the grant. If you are a distant relative, please supply a brief family tree showing your relationship to the deceased person.

Where might the will be stored?

The original will may be held at a solicitor's office or bank, or at the Principal Probate Registry in London. It may be among the deceased person's possessions. If you do not send the original will your application will take longer to deal with.

We will not return the original will to you as it becomes a public record once it has been proved (acted on). We will, however, send you an official copy of the will with the grant of representation.

What if I don't want to apply for a grant and I am named as an executor in a will?

Executors may choose to give up all their rights to a grant ('renunciation') or they may reserve the right, ('power reserved'), to apply for a grant in the future. Unlike renunciation, power reserved will not prevent you applying for a grant at a later date should you need to do so.

Only the executor(s) who swear an oath in support of the application will be named on the grant and only their signature will be required to release the deceased person's assets.

If the person who is entitled to the grant does not wish to apply, they may appoint someone else to be their attorney to obtain the grant on their behalf. If this is the case the details of the person appointing the attorney should be entered on form **PA1**. We will then send you a form for that person to give formal authority, for you to act on their behalf. If the person entitled to the grant has already signed an Enduring Power of Attorney (EPA) or a Lasting Power of Attorney (LPA) please file the original document with your application. This document will be returned to you.

The grant will be issued in the name of the attorney but will state that it is for the "use and benefit" of the person entitled to the grant.

Note – LPA must be registered with the Office of the Public Guardian before it can be used.

You can contact them via www.justice.gov.uk/about/opg or by calling 0845 330 2900.

Why do I need to think about inheritance tax now?

The tax on the estate of a person who has died is called inheritance tax. It is dealt with by HM Revenue & Customs (HMRC). If inheritance tax is due, you normally have to pay at least some of the tax before we can issue the grant.

The issue of the grant does not mean that HMRC have agreed the final inheritance tax liability. They will usually contact you again after you have received the grant. Subject to the requirements to pay some of the tax before obtaining the grant, inheritance tax is due six months after the end of the month in which the person died. HMRC will charge interest on unpaid tax from this due date whatever the reason for late payment.

Probate registry staff are not trained to deal with queries about HMRC forms or inheritance tax. If you have any queries about these you should visit the HMRC website: www.hmrc.gov.uk/inheritancetax or contact the Probate and Inheritance Tax Helpline on 0300 123 1072.

How do I apply for a grant?

You will need to follow the process set out below:

Complete the Probate Service application form

You will need to complete **Probate Application form PA1**, using **Guidance Leaflet PA1A**. You can get these forms by:

- calling the Probate and Inheritance Tax Helpline on 0300 123 1072;
- downloading them from hmctsformfinder.justice.gov.uk. Please note, you cannot save the form online or submit electronically but you can either complete on the screen and print it, or print the blank form and complete it by hand; or
- they can be obtained by email from a probate registry.

Complete the HMRC tax form

When you apply for a grant, you will need to complete a tax form **whether or not inheritance tax is owed**. You should use form **IHT205** if no inheritance tax is payable. If form **IHT205** is not applicable to you, please contact HMRC for form **IHT400**.

For help completing the forms, you can contact the Probate and Inheritance Tax Helpline on 0300 123 1072.

Please note, no grant can issue until either it has been confirmed by you that no inheritance tax is payable, or that, if inheritance tax is payable, HMRC has confirmed to the Probate Service that the grant can issue.

Options for swearing the oath

As part of the application process you will need to swear an oath to confirm the information you have provided in the application form is true to your best knowledge and belief. The oath will also set out the legal requirements expected of you as the holder of the grant. The oath, which is a document containing all the necessary information to support the application, will be prepared for you by Probate Service staff, and you can choose to swear it either:

- at the office of any commissioner for oaths (usually a solicitor's office) convenient to yourself; or
- by attending at one of the probate venues listed in leaflet **PA4** (we will send you the oath and details of how to arrange the appointment).

Please note, it will usually take no more than five minutes to swear the oath. You may wish to take this into consideration when deciding which option you wish to take.

Before a commissioner for oaths

If you choose to go to a commissioner of oaths to swear the oath in support of your application you may be able to swear your papers closer to your home or place of work than if you attend at a probate venue. Commissioners of oaths are often solicitors but they will have no involvement either in your application or the administration of the estate; your only contact with them will be for the formal swearing of the oath – usually no more than five minutes.

The first named applicant will be sent the oath which must then be taken to a solicitor of their choice before whom they wish to swear the oath. All applicants who wish to be named on the grant will be required to swear the oath. We will send further instructions on the process to follow when we send you the oath.

A charge of £10 for each oath and 50p for each exhibit is made by the solicitor for this service. An exhibit is any document referred to in the oath and will usually be a copy of the will (if one was left). You will need to contact the solicitor to make appropriate arrangements to swear the oath. If you are outside England or Wales, different charges may apply and you may wish to check the fee beforehand and also contact the Probate Registry for further information on how to do this.

If you choose this option you should write **'solicitor's office'** in the box labelled **'interview venue'** on the first page of the form **PA1**.

This option may not be applicable in all cases and it may be necessary for you to attend an appointment at the registry. Should this apply in your case, you will be contacted by the Probate Service.

At a probate venue

If you attend a probate venue, there is no additional charge for swearing the oath, and the arrangements for you to swear the oath will be made by probate staff. The leaflet **PA4** provides more information on the locations for swearing the oath if you choose this option.

The locations highlighted in bold on the PA4 have limited opening times, as an appointment date for that venue will only be set once a minimum of 50 applications wishing to attend have been received. When selecting a venue your appointment will be fixed for the next available date. It may be that an earlier date can be given at the main registry and this will be discussed when you call.

If you choose to swear your oath at a probate venue you should write your preferred location in the box labelled **'interview venue'** on the first page of the form **PA1**.

Decide how many official sealed copies of the grant of representation you need

Organisations like banks and building societies need to see sealed copies of the grant before they can release assets to you. They won't accept unsealed photocopies.

Therefore, if you want to deal with the estate quickly, you may want to order enough sealed copies of the grant to send to all the organisations you are dealing with at the same time.

If there are any assets held outside England and Wales, those asset holders may require a copy of the grant to be provided in a different format – usually referred to as a sealed and certified copy.

It is still possible to obtain further sealed copies of the grant for official use after it has issued. You will need to write to the probate registry which issued the grant. However, these will cost more than those ordered at the time of application (see **PA3** – fees list), so it is important to decide before you apply for the grant how many copies you will need.

Make sure you enclose the correct documents

You will need to enclose:

- An official copy (**not** a photocopy) of the death certificate issued by the Registrar of Births Deaths and Marriages or a coroner's certificate.
- The **original** will and any codicils (or any document in which the deceased person expresses any wishes about the distribution of his or her estate). **Keep a copy of any will or codicil you send us**. Please do not attach anything to the will by staple, pin etc. or remove any fastenings from the will.
- Three clear and legible A4 copies of the will and any codicils.

- Any other documents specifically requested by the Probate Service or on the form **PA1**.

- The appropriate HMRC form for your application.

- A cheque made payable to 'HM Courts & Tribunals Service' for the fee, and including the cost of the number of additional copies you have requested. See the fees list on leaflet **PA3**. (We cannot process your application until the fee has been paid.)

Where should I send my application?

You should send your application to the probate registry of your choice (see leaflet **PA4** for the address). You can choose any venue for your appointment to swear the oath, **but your application must be sent to the main Probate Registry responsible for that venue**. You may wish to send your application by registered or recorded post.

Processing the application

When we receive your application, we will examine it and if we have all the information/ documentation to enable us to process your case, we will send you a letter (usually within 10-14 days of receiving your application) acknowledging receipt of your application and providing you with a copy of the oath you will need to swear.

If you have opted to swear the oath at a local solicitor you should contact that solicitor to make appropriate arrangements. We will send further instructions on the process when we send you the oath.

If you have opted to swear the oath at a probate venue, we will send the oath to you and then you can call to arrange a date convenient for you.

If you are applying for a grant with someone else and they cannot come with you, we can arrange for them to swear the oath separately at a different location if necessary. This will, however, increase the time it takes to issue your grant.

We will contact you if, after examining your application, we have any queries. If we do contact you, and you are unable to provide us with the further information and/or documentation we require, it is possible an order may be made that your application is not suitable to be dealt with as a personal application. If this is the case, you will need to instruct a solicitor or probate practitioner to make the application on your behalf.

We may require you to sign additional documents or contact other people – for example, a witness to a will – so that we can interview them or obtain their signatures on documents to help with your application.

What happens when I swear the oath?

You will be asked to sign the prepared oath and to swear, or affirm, before the commissioner of oaths or probate officer that the information you have given is true to the best of your knowledge. You will be given the opportunity to swear on the religious book of your choice.

What happens after I have sworn the oath?

If you have sworn the oath at a local solicitor, you should return it to the registry. Once we have the oath, provided we have all the necessary documentation, we will send you the original grant and copies of the grant (if you have requested them) and return the original death certificate to you, usually within seven working days. You can arrange to collect the documents in person if you want. If you wish to do this, please confirm this in a covering letter when returning the sworn oath.

We retain the original will, as it becomes a public record.

After the grant has issued

When the grant has been issued you will receive information about your role as the executor (**PA97**).

Your duties are to:

- collect the estate (money, property, etc);
- pay debts, funeral expenses etc;
- pay the balance to the persons who are legally entitled to it; and
- keep receipts and a record of what you have done.

You will have the legal right to ask any person or organisation holding the deceased person's assets to give you access to those assets. These assets can then be released, sold or transferred in accordance with the deceased person's wishes or in accordance with the law if the deceased person left no will or codicil(s).

Please note, once issued, all grants of representation, and copy wills which have been proved are public records. Copies of grants and wills can be requested by anyone, on payment of the appropriate fee (see **PA3**).

The responsibility of the Probate Service ends when the grant is issued, and we cannot advise you on how to administer the estate. If you have any questions about this, you may wish to take legal advice.

Useful contacts

For general information on wills and probate:
www.gov.uk/wills-probate-inheritance/overview

To access the online forms and leaflets:
hmctsformfinder.justice.gov.uk

To find the addresses of the regional probate registries:
courttribunalfinder.service.gov.uk/

For information about inheritance tax and online forms:
www.hmrc.gov.uk/inheritancetax

For more detailed information about probate and inheritance tax:
Probate and Inheritance Tax Helpline: 0300 123 1072

Probate forms and leaflets

PA1   Probate application form

PA1A Probate application form
(guidance notes)

PA2   How to obtain probate (leaflet)

PA3   Probate fees list (leaflet)

PA4   Directory of probate registries and interview venues (leaflet)

PA7   How to deposit a will with the
Probate Service (leaflet)

PA7A Withdrawing your will from the
Principal Probate Registry (form)

PA8   How to enter a caveat (leaflet)

PA8A How to enter a caveat (form)

PA9   How to enter a general search (leaflet)

PA10 How to enter a standing search (leaflet)

PA1S Application for a Probate Search or Standing Search (form)

HMRC Inheritance Tax forms

IHT205 Return of estate information

IHT206 Return of estate information (guidance notes)

IHT400 Inheritance Tax Account

Probate Fees from April 2014

	Fee
Application In all cases where the net estate (ie the amount remaining in the deceased's sole name after funeral expenses and debts owing have been deducted) is **over £5,000** (see example 1 below). **Note: Joint assets passing automatically to the surviving joint owner should not be included when calculating the fee.**	£215
If the net estate as above is **under £5,000** (see example 2 below).	No fee
Application for a second grant in an estate where a previous grant has been issued.	£20
Additional Copies Official (sealed) copies of the Grant of Representation **if** ordered when you lodge your application for a Grant of Representation. **Note: You should decide how many copies you will need and add the cost to your application fee – this will give you the total amount payable. See examples below. It can save you a lot of time when collecting in the deceased's assets if you have a few extra copies of the grant to produce to the organisations holding the assets.**	50p per copy
'Sealed and certified copy' – if assets are held abroad you may need one of these. Please check with the appropriate organisations before ordering.	50p per copy (including Will and Grant)
Additional copies (consisting of grant including a copy of the Will, if applicable) ordered after the Grant of Representation has been issued.	£10 for first copy then 50p per additional copy

Example 1				Example 2			
Net estate of £75,000	=	Fee	£215	Net estate of £2,000	=	Fee	Nil
4 copies of grant at 50p	=	Fee	£ 2	1 copy of grant at 50p	=	Fee	50p
each		Total Fee	£217	each		Total Fee	50p

Please send a cheque or postal order (no cash) made payable to '**HM Courts & Tribunals Service**', together with your application forms, to the Probate Registry to which you are applying. You should state the number and type of copies you need on the checklist on page 4 of the PA1 (application form). Please print the name of the **deceased person** on the back of the cheque.

Please ensure you order sufficient copies for your needs, when you send in your application.

Please note: Appropriate post must be paid. (Standard rate postage may not be sufficient. If your forms weigh over 60g they may need to be weighed at your local Post Office.)

What if I cannot afford to pay a fee?

If you cannot afford the fee, you may be eligible for a fee remission in full or part. The combined booklet and application form EX160A - Court fees - do I have to pay them? gives all the information you need. You can get a copy from any Probate Registry or from our website www.hmcourts-service.gov.uk.

Your application will not be processed until the fee is paid (or an application for refund/remission has been successful).

HM Courts & Tribunals Service

Directory of Probate Registries and Appointment Venues

For general enquiries, please telephone the Probate and Inheritance Tax Helpline Monday to Friday 9am to 5pm on 0300 123 1072.

The main Probate Registries are open to the public 9.30 am to 4.00 pm Monday to Friday. London is open from 10am to 4.30pm Monday to Friday.

Further information regarding making an appointment to swear your oath will be sent to you by the Probate Registry after you submit your application.

Please note: There is now also an option for you to have your appointment before a commissioner for oaths at a solicitor's office of your choice. Full details of this will also be sent at this stage.

Whichever option you choose your application **must** be sent to the main Probate Registry.

If you have any questions you may contact the Probate Helpline on 0300 123 1072.

Main Probate Registry:	Appointment venues:	Please note: Opening times of offices marked in bold vary and can be limited. You will be advised of this when we receive your application.
Birmingham Probate Registry The Priory Courts 33 Bull Street Birmingham B4 6DU Tel: 0121 681 3400/3414	Birmingham **Nottingham** **Stoke-on-Trent**	
Brighton Probate Registry William Street Brighton BN2 0RF Tel: 01273 573510	Brighton	
Bristol Probate Registry The Civil Justice Centre 2 Redcliff Street Bristol BS1 6GR Tel: 0117 3664960/61	Bristol **Bodmin** **Exeter**	
Cardiff **Probate Registry of Wales** 3rd Floor, Cardiff Magistrates' Court Fitzalan Place, Cardiff South Wales CF24 0RZ Tel: 02920 474373	Cardiff **Caernarfon** **Carmarthen**	
Ipswich Probate Registry Ground Floor 8 Arcade Street Ipswich IP1 1EJ Tel: 01473 284260	Ipswich Norwich **Peterborough**	

Main Probate Registry:	Appointment venues:
Leeds Probate Registry York House York Place Leeds LS1 2BA Tel: 0113 3896 133	Leeds Lincoln **York**
Liverpool Probate Registry The Queen Elizabeth II Law Courts Derby Square Liverpool L2 1XA Tel: 0151 236 8264	Liverpool **Chester** **Lancaster**
London Probate Department Principal Registry of the Family Division First Avenue House 42-49 High Holborn London WC1V 6NP Tel: 020 7421 8500/8509	Central London
Manchester Probate Registry Manchester Civil Justice Centre Ground Floor 1 Bridge Street West PO Box 4240 Manchester M60 1WJ Tel: 0161 240 5701/5702	Manchester
Newcastle-Upon-Tyne Probate Registry Newcastle DPR No 1 Waterloo Square Newcastle-Upon-Tyne NE1 4DR Tel: 0191 211 2170	Newcastle-Upon-Tyne **Carlisle** **Middlesbrough**
Oxford Probate Registry Combined Court Building St Aldates Oxford OX1 1LY Tel: 01865 793055	Oxford **Gloucester** **Leicester**
Sheffield Probate Registry PO Box 832 The Law Courts 50 West Bar Sheffield S3 8YR Tel: 0114 281 2596	Sheffield
Winchester Probate Registry 4th Floor Cromwell House Andover Road Winchester SO23 7EW Tel: 01962 897029	Winchester